new curries

INDIA • SRI LANKA • THAILAND • MALAYSIA • INDONESIA • VIETNAM

THE AUSTRALIAN
Women's Weekly

contents

Not only is a good curry something to enjoy with relish, but it's also an easy-to-make one-dish main meal that's as perfect for entertaining as it is for the family dinner. Deliciously spicy Thai and Malaysian curries today share the spotlight with their Indian and Pakistani counterparts on our red-carpet list of new favourite recipes.

Pamela Clark

Food Director

currying flavour

The fragrant aroma of a curry wafting from the kitchen stove stimulates the appetite and evokes memories of meals savoured in many an Indian eatery over the years, as well as those enjoyed more recently in Malaysian, Thai and Vietnamese restaurants. As food lovers, we've embraced curries, no matter what their country of origin, as one of our favourite foods, and one we like to make at home: here you'll find a selection of those that may have been born anywhere from Burma to the Caribbean, but which have been adopted with love as our own.

Generally accepted as originating from kari, a Tamil word for a spicy or seasonal gravy or sauce, a curry is basically just that; while the recipes vary from country to country, and even region to region, most share the common denominator of being wet and savoury. From an incendiary Goan vindaloo to a mellow Kenyan stew, from traditional robust lamb and chicken mixtures to lighter seafood and vegetable dishes new to our repertoires, there's a curry to suit all tastebuds and occasions.

Whether you use prepared curry paste or make your own, it's most important that it be of a very high standard, an amalgam of herbs, aromatic spices, dried and fresh chillies and, on occasion, fruits, seafood, stems, roots or nuts, crushed or ground together to make a complex, intensely flavoured ingredient.

Accompanied by a fluffy rice dish or a homemade bread, a tasty relish or dipping sauce, and a platter of cooling fresh greens or a bowl of raita, a curry is a perfect main dish to lend an exotic spin to any meal.

TIPS FOR THE COOK MAKING A CURRY

• Use cheaper meat cuts if you have the time to cook a curry a long while; go for the more tender (and expensive) cuts if time is of the essence.
• Many curries benefit from being cooked one day and eaten the next, allowing the flavours to meld into an aromatic whole overnight.
• Store dried spices in airtight containers in the refrigerator or freezer to maintain freshness; freeze any remaining curry pastes for future use.
• There is no need to separate the seeds from a cardamom pod: simply crush the husk with the side of a heavy knife to expose the seeds. Some cooks remove the husks just before serving, but it's not mandatory.

4

curry ingredients

BANANA LEAVES can be ordered from fruit and vegetable stores. Cut them with a sharp knife close to the main stem then immerse in hot water to make leaves pliable. *(see page 11)*

BLACK CUMIN SEEDS also known as jeera kala; often confused with kalonji (black onion or nigella seeds). Imparts a distinctive "curry" flavour to dishes.

CARDAMOM one of the world's most expensive spices; has a distinctive aromatic, sweetly rich flavour. Purchase in pod, seed or ground form.

CINNAMON STICK dried inner bark of the shoots of the cinnamon tree; the stick, once ground, is what we use as cinnamon powder.

CORIANDER also known as pak chee, cilantro or chinese parsley; bright-green-leafed herb with a pungent flavour. Stems and roots of coriander are also used in South-East Asian cooking; wash well before chopping. Coriander is also available as seeds and in ground form; these must never be used to replace fresh coriander, or vice versa, as the tastes are completely different. *(see page 12)*

CURRY
leaves available fresh and dried; buy fresh leaves at Indian food shops. Used to give extra flavour and depth to curries. *(see page 16)*

powder a blend of various ground spices; may include dried chilli, cumin, cinnamon, coriander, fennel, fenugreek, mace, cardamom and turmeric. Choose mild or hot to suit your taste.

EGGPLANT also known as aubergine or brinjal; ranges in size from tiny to very large and in colour from pale green to deep purple.
pea also known as makeua puong, slightly larger than a green pea and of similar shape and colour; sold fresh, in bunches like grapes, or pickled packed in jars. Available in Asian grocery stores. *(see page 24)*
thai also known as makeua prao, golf-ball sized eggplants available in different colours but most commonly green traced in off-white. They have bitter seeds that must be removed before using. *(see below)*

FENUGREEK hard, dried seed of the aromatic plant native to Asia and southern Europe; has a pleasantly bitter, yet slightly sweet, taste.

FISH SAUCE called naam pla or nuoc naam. Made from pulverised salted fermented fish (most often anchovies); has a pungent smell and strong taste, Use according to your taste.

GALANGAL
fresh also known as ka, a rhizome with a hot ginger-citrusy flavour; used similarly to ginger. *(see below)*

pickled also known as ka dong, is used both in cooking and as a condiment served with various noodle and chicken dishes. It is sold cryovac-packed or in jars in Asian grocery stores.

GARAM MASALA a blend of spices, originating in North India. Used as a basis for a curry paste or on its own sprinkled over dishes.

GHEE clarified butter with the milk solids removed; this fat can be heated to a high temperature without burning. *(see page 7)*

KAFFIR LIME LEAVES also known as bai magrood; look like two glossy dark green leaves joined end to end, forming a rounded hourglass shape. Sold fresh, dried or frozen, the dried leaves are less potent so double the number called for in a recipe if you substitute them for fresh leaves. A strip of fresh lime peel can be substituted for each kaffir lime leaf. *(see page 19)*

KECAP ASIN an astringent, salty, soy-sauce-based ketchup used in Indonesian recipes.

KECAP MANIS called sieu wan in Thai; a dark, thick, sweet soy sauce used in most South-East Asian cuisines. The soy's sweetness is derived from the addition of either molasses or palm sugar when brewed.

shrimp paste

thai eggplant

tamarind

galangal

LEMON GRASS a tall, clumping, sharp-edged aromatic tropical grass that both smells and tastes of lemon, can be found fresh, dried, powdered and frozen in supermarkets and greengrocers as well as Asian food shops. Its refreshingly light taste is less citric or "bitey" than lemon, and carries with it a hint of ginger; however, its similarity to lemon means it marries well with chilli, garlic and coriander. *(see page 28)*

OKRA also known as bamia, bhindi or lady fingers; a green, ridged, oblong pod with a furry skin used to thicken stews. *(see page 87)*

PALM SUGAR also known as nam tan pip, jaggery, jawa or gula melaka; made from the sap of the sugar palm tree. Light brown to black in colour; usually sold in rock-hard cakes. Substitute brown sugar, if unavailable. *(see below)*

PANEER a simple, delicate fresh cow-milk cheese used as a major source of protein in the Indian diet. Ricotta can be substituted. *(see page 84)*

PASTES
many curry pastes are available in supermarkets. Green curry paste is one of the most popular Thai pastes – along with red, massaman, panang and yellow. Curry pastes are generally used as the basis for curry dishes; may also be made at home using fresh ingredients.

green the hottest of the traditional pastes; contains chilli, garlic, onion, lemon grass, spice, salt, galangal.
korma a rich, mild sauce with a delicate coconut flavour and hints of garlic, ginger and coriander.
rogan josh a paste of medium heat made from fresh chillies or paprika, tomato and spices. *(see page 56)*
tandoori a paste of medium heat consisting of garlic, tamarind, ginger, coriander, chilli and spices.
shrimp also known as kapi, trasi and blanchan; a strong-scented, very firm preserved paste made of salted dried shrimp. Also sold in slabs or flat cakes, which should be chopped or sliced thinly then wrapped in foil and roasted before use. *(see page 6)*

PICKLED GREEN PEPPERCORNS (prik tai ahn) have a fresh herbal "green" flavour without being extremely pungent; early-harvested unripe pepper that needs to be dried or pickled to avoid fermentation. We used pickled thai green peppercorns, which are canned, still strung in clusters but you can use an equivalent weight from a bottle of green peppercorns in brine. *(see page 15)*

PURPLE SHALLOTS also known as pink or asian shallots or homm; eaten fresh, deep-fried as a condiment, pounded in curry pastes or tossed into stir-fries.

TAMARIND brown "hairy" pods from the tamarind tree filled with seeds and a viscous pulp that are dried and pressed into blocks of tamarind. Gives a sweet-sour, slightly astringent taste to food. Found in Asian supermarkets. *(see page 6)*

TAMARIND CONCENTRATE (or paste) the commercial distillation of tamarind juice into a condensed, compacted paste. Thick and purplish-black, it is ready to use, with no soaking or straining required; dilute paste with water according to taste.

THAI BASIL has smallish leaves, and sweet licorice/aniseed taste; available in Asian supermarkets and greengrocers. *(see below)*

TURMERIC also known as kamin; must be grated or pounded before use. Fresh turmeric can be substituted with the more common dried powder: use 2 teaspoons of ground turmeric plus a teaspoon of sugar for every 20g of fresh turmeric called for in a recipe. *(see page 20)*

SAMBAL OELEK (also ulek or olek) Indonesian in origin; a salty paste made from ground chillies.

VIETNAMESE MINT not actually a mint, but a pungent and peppery narrow-leafed member of the buckwheat family. *(see below)*

thai basil

vietnamese mint

palm sugar

ghee

seafood

We're lucky to live in a country where a variety of fresh, high-quality seafood is readily available. The subtle, delicate flavours of fish, prawns and crabs are enhanced by the addition of aromatic spices and highly fragrant herbs to create curries that delight all senses.

sri lankan crab curry

1 tablespoon peanut oil
2 large brown onions (400g), chopped finely
4 cloves garlic, crushed
3cm piece fresh ginger (15g), grated
1 fresh small red thai chilli, chopped finely
4 dried curry leaves
½ teaspoon fenugreek seeds
1 teaspoon ground cinnamon
1 teaspoon ground turmeric
2 x 400ml cans coconut cream
1 tablespoon fish sauce
2 tablespoons lime juice
2 whole cooked mud crabs (1.6kg)
½ cup (25g) coconut flakes, toasted

1 Heat oil in wok; stir-fry onion, garlic, ginger and chilli until onion softens. Add curry leaves and spices; stir-fry until fragrant. Add coconut cream, sauce and juice; simmer, uncovered, 30 minutes.
2 Meanwhile, prepare crabs. Lift tail flap of each crab then, with a peeling motion, lift off the back of each shell. Remove and discard the gills, liver and brain matter; rinse crabs well. Cut each body in half; separate claws from bodies. You will have eight pieces.
3 Add half of the crab to wok; simmer, covered, about 10 minutes or until crab is heated through. Transfer crab to large serving bowl; cover to keep warm. Repeat with remaining crab pieces.
4 Spoon curry sauce over crab; sprinkle with coconut.
TIP If you use uncooked crabs, increase the cooking time of the crabs by about 15 minutes; cook until they change colour.
__ per serving 52.5g total fat (37.2g saturated fat); 3118kJ (746 cal); 14.4g carbohydrate; 51.9g protein; 6.4g fibre

Sweet-fleshed crabs are plentiful on the island nation of Sri Lanka, and there are myriad recipes using them as the focus in a luscious curry – this is one of our favourites. Blue swimmer or spanner crabs can also be used for this recipe.

preparation time 30 minutes cooking time 55 minutes serves 4

snapper wrapped in banana leaves

1 Combine paste, tamarind and the water in large bowl; add fish, turn fish to coat in mixture. Stir in ginger, onion, chilli, carrot and snow peas. Cover; refrigerate 3 hours or overnight.
2 Trim one leaf into four 25cm squares. Place squares, dull-side down, on heated grill plate about 1 minute or until pliable. Trim remaining leaf to fit grill plate.
3 Place one fish on each banana leaf square; top with vegetable mixture, sprinkle each with coriander. Fold two opposing corners of leaf over filling then fold remaining pair of corners over to enclose filling. Secure parcels with kitchen string.
4 Place trimmed banana leaf on heated grill plate (or grill or barbecue); place parcels on leaf. Cook, covered with foil (or an inverted flameproof baking dish), about 20 minutes or until fish is cooked as desired.
__ per serving 6g total fat (1.9g saturated fat); 1367kJ (327 cal); 7.7g carbohydrate; 57.9g protein; 3.8g fibre

¼ cup (75g) red curry paste (page 110)
1 tablespoon tamarind concentrate
1 tablespoon water
4 snapper fillets (1.1kg)
5cm piece fresh ginger (25g), cut
   into matchsticks
2 green onions, sliced thinly
2 fresh small red chillies, sliced thinly
2 large carrots (360g), sliced thinly
100g snow peas, trimmed, sliced thinly
2 large banana leaves
½ cup loosely packed fresh coriander leaves

In Indonesia, particularly on Java, food is often wrapped in banana leaves before steaming or grilling a process called "pepesan", which gives a special flavour to the food. The leaves are either par-boiled or made pliable over high heat before use. Fresh banana leaves are available in greengrocers and some large supermarkets. You can use a prepared curry paste for this recipe, if you prefer.

preparation time 20 minutes (plus refrigeration time) cooking time 20 minutes serves 4

chilli king prawn skewers with pistachio coriander rub

32 uncooked large king prawns (2.2kg)
1 teaspoon ground turmeric
1 teaspoon cumin seeds
1 tablespoon coriander seeds
¼ teaspoon chilli flakes
2 long green chillies, chopped coarsely
2 tablespoons desiccated coconut
2cm piece fresh ginger (10g), grated
2 tablespoons blanched almonds, roasted
2 tablespoons pistachios, roasted
140ml can coconut milk
1 tablespoon vegetable oil
1 tablespoon warm water
2 tablespoons fresh coriander leaves

1   Shell and devein prawns. Thread four prawns onto each skewer.
2   Blend or process spices, green chilli, coconut, ginger, nuts, coconut milk and oil until mixture forms a paste. Transfer to small bowl; stir in the water.
3   Rub paste into prawns; cook skewers on heated oiled grill plate (or grill or barbecue), brushing occasionally with remaining paste, until prawns are changed in colour and cooked.
4   Serve skewers sprinkled with coriander leaves.
__ per serving 22.2g total fat (9.5g saturated fat); 1906kJ (456 cal); 2.9g carbohydrate; 60g protein; 2.4g fibre

Coriander is said to be one of the world's most-used herbs, and you'll find it starring uncooked in pestos, salsas and salads just as often as it is stirred into stir-fries, curries and chutneys. The flavour of fresh coriander and its seeds dominate this dish.
You need to soak eight bamboo skewers in water for at least an hour before using to prevent them splintering and scorching.

preparation time 45 minutes cooking time 10 minutes serves 4

fish ball and
green peppercorn red curry

1   Blend or process fish, garlic, soy sauce, cornflour, coriander mixture and ginger until mixture forms a paste; roll level tablespoons of mixture into balls.

2   Cook oil and curry paste in large saucepan, stirring, until fragrant. Gradually stir in coconut milk; simmer, uncovered, 5 minutes. Add fish balls, peppercorn stems, sugar, lime leaves, fish sauce and corn; cook, uncovered, about 5 minutes or until fish balls are cooked through.

3   Serve curry sprinkled with sprouts, chilli and coriander leaves.

TIPS Keep uncooked fish balls, covered, in single layer on tray, in the refrigerator until required. The fish balls will firm up and the flavours of the mixture will blend together. You can also freeze uncooked fish balls in snap-lock plastic bags.

___ per serving 47.6g total fat (37.3g saturated fat); 2972kJ (711 cal); 23.4g carbohydrate; 44.7g protein; 7.2g fibre

750g firm white fish fillets, chopped coarsely
3 cloves garlic, quartered
2 tablespoons soy sauce
2 tablespoons cornflour
2 tablespoons finely chopped
   coriander root and stem mixture
2cm piece fresh ginger (10g), grated
2 teaspoons peanut oil
⅓ cup (100g) red curry paste (page 110)
2 x 400g cans coconut milk
4 x 5cm stems pickled green
   peppercorns (20g), rinsed, drained
2 teaspoons grated palm sugar
2 fresh kaffir lime leaves, shredded finely
2 teaspoons fish sauce
115g baby corn, halved lengthways
1 cup bean sprouts (80g)
1 fresh long red chilli, sliced thinly
¼ cup loosely packed fresh coriander leaves

Pickled green peppercorns are less pungent than black peppercorns and are frequently used in Thai curries. Preserved on the stem in brine, they can be found in Asian food stores. You can substitute french green peppercorns, if necessary.

preparation time 30 minutes cooking time 15 minutes serves 4

assamese sour fish curry

1 tablespoon coriander seeds
2 teaspoons cumin seeds
½ teaspoon ground turmeric
1 teaspoon black peppercorns
2cm piece fresh ginger (10g),
  chopped coarsely
2 cloves garlic, chopped coarsely
2 long green chillies, chopped coarsely
2 tablespoons vegetable oil
4 blue-eye cutlets (800g)
2 medium brown onions (300g),
  sliced thinly
1½ teaspoons black mustard seeds
4 fresh curry leaves
¾ cup (180ml) water
⅓ cup (80ml) fish stock
¼ cup (60ml) lime juice
1 tablespoon fish sauce

1 Dry-fry coriander and cumin seeds and turmeric in small frying pan, stirring, until fragrant. Using mortar and pestle, crush spices with peppercorns, ginger, garlic and chilli to form a paste.
2 Heat half of the oil in large frying pan; cook fish, uncovered, until browned both sides. Remove from pan; cover to keep warm.
3 Heat remaining oil in same pan; cook onion, mustard seeds and curry leaves, stirring, about 5 minutes or until onion is browned lightly. Add spice paste; cook, stirring, until fragrant. Add the water, stock, juice and sauce; bring to a boil. Return fish to the pan; simmer, covered, about 5 minutes or until fish is cooked as desired.
__ per serving 12.9g total fat (2.3g saturated fat); 1150kJ (275 cal); 3.8g carbohydrate; 34.7g protein; 1.6g fibre

Assam is a landlocked state in the northeast of India; however, it's on the Ganges flood plain and much of its inhabitants' staple diet consists of river fish. We used blue-eye here, but replace it with whatever firm, full-flavoured fish you like. Curry leaves are used in many Indian recipes, and add extra depth and flavour to curries.

preparation time 20 minutes cooking time 20 minutes serves 4

panang fish curry

1   Place coconut milk, paste, sauce, sugar and lime leaves in wok; simmer, stirring, about 15 minutes or until mixture reduces by a third.
2   Meanwhile, heat oil in large frying pan; cook seafood, in batches, until just changed in colour. Drain on absorbent paper.
3   Add beans and seafood to curry mixture; cook, uncovered, stirring occasionally, about 5 minutes or until beans are just tender and seafood is cooked as desired.
4   Serve curry sprinkled with basil, nuts and chilli.
—   per serving 64.3g total fat (39.8g saturated fat); 3716kJ (889 cal); 18.3g carbohydrate; 57.1g protein; 7.2g fibre

2 x 400ml cans coconut milk
¼ cup (60g) panang curry paste (page 111)
¼ cup (60ml) fish sauce
2 tablespoons grated palm sugar
4 fresh kaffir lime leaves, torn
2 tablespoons peanut oil
500g ling fillets, cut into 3cm pieces
500g uncooked medium king prawns
250g scallops
200g snake beans, chopped coarsely
½ cup loosely packed fresh thai basil leaves
½ cup (70g) coarsely chopped roasted
   unsalted peanuts
2 fresh long red chillies, sliced thinly

This curry has its origins in the curries of Penang, an island off the northwest coast of Malaysia, close to the Thai border. The paste is a complex, sweet and milder variation of an authentic Thai red curry paste, which is especially good with seafood. Kaffir lime leaves, aromatic leaves of a citrus tree, are used similarly to bay leaves or curry leaves. They are available from Asian food stores.

preparation time 15 minutes cooking time 30 minutes serves 4

fish yellow curry

8 baby new potatoes (320g), halved
400ml can coconut milk
¼ cup (70g) yellow curry paste (page 111)
¼ cup (60ml) fish stock
2 tablespoons fish sauce
1 tablespoon lime juice
1 tablespoon grated palm sugar
800g firm white fish fillets, cut into
  3cm pieces
3 green onions, sliced thinly
⅓ cup coarsely chopped fresh coriander
1 fresh long red chilli, sliced thinly
1 tablespoon finely chopped
  fresh coriander

1 Boil, steam or microwave potato until just tender; drain.
2 Meanwhile, place half of the coconut milk in large saucepan; bring to a boil. Boil, stirring, until milk reduces by half and the oil separates from the coconut milk. Add curry paste; cook, stirring, about 1 minute or until fragrant. Add remaining coconut milk, stock, sauce, juice and sugar; cook, stirring, until sugar dissolves.
3 Add fish and potato to pan; cook, covered, about 3 minutes or until fish is cooked. Stir in onion and coarsely chopped coriander.
4 Divide curry among serving bowls; sprinkle with chilli and finely chopped coriander.
__ per serving 23g total fat (18.5g saturated fat); 1960kJ (469 cal); 18.9g carbohydrate; 44.7g protein; 3.9g fibre

Yellow curry paste is a fairly mild curry paste and, because of the inclusion of turmeric, is the one that most closely resembles an Indian curry in flavour.
This particular fish curry, too, is not unlike some of the curries found on the west coast of India, those from Goa or Kerala, areas from which traders sailed east, taking many of their culinary influences to Thailand.

preparation time 20 minutes cooking time 20 minutes serves 4

dry thai prawn curry

1 Place dried chillies in small heatproof jug, cover with boiling water; stand 15 minutes, drain.

2 Shell and devein prawns, leaving tails intact.

3 Blend or process soaked chillies, galangal, lemon grass, coriander mixture, garlic, paste, half of the oil and half of the lime leaf until mixture forms a paste.

4 Transfer curry paste mixture to large bowl, add prawns; mix well.

5 Heat remaining oil in wok; stir-fry prawn mixture with remaining lime leaf until prawns are changed in colour. Add the water, sauce and sugar; stir-fry 1 minute. Remove from heat; toss apple, shallot, coriander leaves and fresh chilli into curry.

___ per serving 10.6g total fat (1.4g saturated fat); 1183kJ (283 cal); 6.1g carbohydrate; 40g protein; 1.5g fibre

5 dried long red chillies

1.5kg uncooked medium prawns

2 tablespoons coarsely chopped fresh galangal

10cm stick (20g) fresh lemon grass, chopped coarsely

2 tablespoons coarsely chopped coriander root and stem mixture

2 cloves garlic, crushed

1 teaspoon shrimp paste

2 tablespoons vegetable oil

8 fresh kaffir lime leaves, torn

2 tablespoons water

1 tablespoon fish sauce

1 teaspoon caster sugar

1 medium green apple (150g), unpeeled, cut into matchsticks

2 shallots (50g), sliced thinly

½ cup firmly packed fresh coriander leaves

2 fresh long red chillies, sliced thinly

preparation time 10 minutes (plus standing time) **cooking time** 15 minutes **serves** 4

poultry

Poultry has a lot going for it – it's versatile, full of protein, inexpensive as a rule and eaten by people in almost every country in the world. Its delicate simplicity provides the perfect backdrop for any number of different spicy and pungent curry flavours.

chicken green curry

1 tablespoon peanut oil
¼ cup (75g) green curry paste (page 110)
3 long green chillies, chopped finely
1kg chicken thigh fillets, cut into
   3cm pieces
2 x 400ml cans coconut milk
2 tablespoons fish sauce
2 tablespoons lime juice
1 tablespoon grated palm sugar
150g pea eggplants
1 large zucchini (150g), sliced thinly
⅓ cup loosely packed fresh thai basil leaves
¼ cup loosely packed fresh
   coriander leaves
2 green onions, chopped coarsely

1 Heat oil in large saucepan; cook paste and about two-thirds of the chilli, stirring, about 2 minutes or until fragrant. Add chicken; cook, stirring, until browned.
2 Add coconut milk, sauce, juice, sugar and eggplants; simmer, uncovered, about 10 minutes or until eggplants are just tender.
3 Add zucchini, basil and coriander; simmer, uncovered, until zucchini is just tender.
4 Serve curry sprinkled with remaining chilli and green onion.
__ per serving 67.3g total fat (43.2g saturated fat); 3716kJ (889 cal); 17g carbohydrate; 52.9g protein; 6g fibre

Green curry paste is one of the hottest of the Thai traditional pastes, but this doesn't stop it being one of the favourite curries among non-Thai cooks and diners. Here, the coconut milk tempers the fire, but doesn't dilute the beautiful and immediately identifiable flavour of this curry. There are jars of green curry paste available in most supermarkets that you can use instead of making our recipe. Pea eggplants can be found in Asian supermarkets and specialist greengrocers.

preparation time 20 minutes cooking time 30 minutes serves 4

butter chicken

1 Dry-fry nuts, garam masala, coriander and chilli in small frying pan, stirring, until nuts are browned lightly.
2 Blend or process nut mixture with garlic, ginger, vinegar, paste and half the yogurt until mixture forms a paste. Transfer to large bowl, stir in remaining yogurt and chicken. Cover; refrigerate 3 hours or overnight.
3 Melt butter in large saucepan; cook onion, cinnamon and cardamom, stirring, until onion is browned lightly. Add chicken mixture; cook, stirring, 10 minutes.
4 Stir in paprika, puree and stock; simmer, uncovered, 45 minutes, stirring occasionally.
5 Discard cinnamon and cardamom. Add cream; simmer, uncovered, 5 minutes.
__ per serving 74g total fat (33.3g saturated fat); 4138kJ (990 cal); 20.8g carbohydrate; 59.3g protein; 6.5g fibre

1 cup (150g) unsalted raw cashews
2 teaspoons garam masala (page 112)
2 teaspoons ground coriander
½ teaspoon chilli powder
3 cloves garlic, chopped coarsely
4cm piece fresh ginger (20g), grated
2 tablespoons white vinegar
⅓ cup (95g) tomato paste
½ cup (140g) yogurt
1kg chicken thigh fillets, halved
80g butter
1 large brown onion (200g), chopped finely
1 cinnamon stick
4 cardamom pods, bruised
1 teaspoon hot paprika
400g can tomato puree
¾ cup (180ml) chicken stock
¾ cup (180ml) cream

Butter chicken (or murgh makhani), popular in countries with a tradition of Indian restaurants such as Britain and Australia, is tomato-based and quite rich, the addition of cream and butter giving it a thick, velvety texture. Be certain to use unsalted cashews in the roasted curry mixture or the taste of the finished butter chicken may not be as mellow as it could be.

preparation time 30 minutes (plus refrigeration time) cooking time 1 hour 10 minutes serves 4

lemon grass chicken curry

1 tablespoon vegetable oil
24 chicken drumettes (1.7kg)
1 medium brown onion (150g), sliced thinly
3 cloves garlic, crushed
½ teaspoon cracked black pepper
3 x 10cm sticks (60g) fresh lemon grass,
  chopped finely
1 long green chilli, chopped finely
¼ cup (75g) mild curry paste
1 tablespoon grated palm sugar
½ cup (125ml) chicken stock
½ cup (125ml) water
1 medium red capsicum (200g), sliced thinly
1 medium carrot (120g), cut into matchsticks
4 green onions, sliced thinly

1 Heat oil in large flameproof casserole dish; cook chicken, in batches, until browned. Drain and discard cooking juices.
2 Cook brown onion, garlic, pepper, lemon grass and chilli in same pan, stirring, until onion softens. Add paste; cook, stirring, until fragrant. Return chicken to dish; cook, stirring, 5 minutes.
3 Add sugar, stock and the water; cook, covered, 10 minutes. Uncover; simmer about 10 minutes or until chicken is cooked through. Remove chicken from dish; cover to keep warm. Add capsicum and carrot; cook, uncovered, about 5 minutes or until curry sauce thickens and vegetables are just tender. Stir green onion into curry off the heat.
4 Serve chicken topped with curried vegetable mixture.
__ per serving 36.3g total fat (9g saturated fat); 2286kJ (547 cal); 9.9g carbohydrate; 43.8g protein; 4.3g fibre

There are many prepared curry pastes sold in supermarkets, but they vary in flavour, heat and intensity from maker to maker. By and large, however, a rule of thumb to consider is that the milder ones are most likely to be called korma, tikka, panang or yellow; medium pastes can be labelled balti, tandoori, rogan josh, leang or red; while the hotter versions are sold as vindaloo, madras, extra hot, green or crying tiger. Lemon grass, a tall, clumping, lemon-smelling and tasting, sharp-edged grass, is available from supermarkets, Asian food shops and greengrocers.

preparation time 25 minutes cooking time 45 minutes serves 4

duck jungle curry

1   Discard neck then wash duck inside and out; pat dry with absorbent paper. Using sharp knife, separate drumstick and thigh sections from body; separate thighs from drumsticks. Remove and discard wings. Separate breast and backbone; cut breast from bone. You will have six pieces. Cut duck carcass into four pieces; discard any fat from carcass.

2   Heat 1 tablespoon of the oil in large saucepan; cook carcass pieces, stirring occasionally, about 5 minutes or until browned. Add onion, chopped carrot, garlic and ginger; cook, stirring, about 2 minutes or until onion softens. Add black peppercorns, the water and four of the lime leaves; simmer, uncovered, 1 hour 15 minutes, skimming fat from surface of mixture regularly.

3   Strain mixture through muslin-lined sieve into large heatproof jug. Reserve 3 cups of liquid; discard solids and remaining liquid.

4   Preheat oven to moderately hot (200°C/180°C fan-forced). Heat remaining oil in same cleaned pan; cook thighs, drumsticks and breasts, in batches, until browned. Remove skin from breasts and legs; slice skin thinly. Place sliced duck skin on oven tray; roast, uncovered, about 10 minutes or until crisp.

5   Discard excess oil from pan; reheat pan, cook curry paste, stirring, about 1 minute or until fragrant. Add eggplant, sliced carrot, beans, bamboo shoots, green peppercorns, half of the basil, remaining lime leaf and reserved liquid; simmer, uncovered, 5 minutes. Add duck pieces; simmer, uncovered, about 10 minutes or until vegetables are tender. Stir in chilli and sauce.

6   Place curry in serving bowls; sprinkle with remaining basil and crisped duck skin.

__ per serving 121g total fat (34.4g saturated fat); 5334kJ (1276 cal); 8.1g carbohydrate; 41g protein; 5.4g fibre

2kg duck
¼ cup (60ml) peanut oil
1 medium brown onion (150g), chopped coarsely
1 medium carrot (120g), chopped coarsely
2 cloves garlic, halved
4cm piece fresh ginger (20g), sliced thickly
½ teaspoon black peppercorns
2 litres (8 cups) cold water
5 fresh kaffir lime leaves, torn
¼ cup (75g) red curry paste (page 110)
150g thai eggplants, halved
1 medium carrot (120g), sliced thinly
100g snake beans, cut into 4cm lengths
230g can bamboo shoots, rinsed, drained
2 x 5cm stems (10g) pickled green peppercorns
½ cup firmly packed fresh thai basil leaves
4 fresh small red thai chillies, chopped coarsely
2 tablespoons fish sauce

Jungle curry got its name from its place of origin, the central-north region of Thailand, where cooks didn't have access to the coconut trees of the southern coast. It is quite hot and spicy, since no soothing coconut milk or cream are among the ingredients to fight the fire. It calls for Thai eggplants, which are quite hard, pale green in colour and about the size of a golf ball.

preparation time 40 minutes cooking time 2 hours serves 4

chicken in yogurt

2 teaspoons ground cumin

2 teaspoons ground cardamom

1 teaspoon ground cinnamon

½ teaspoon ground clove

½ teaspoon ground turmeric

½ cup (80g) blanched almonds

2cm piece fresh ginger (10g),
chopped coarsely

2 cloves garlic, quartered

500g yogurt

8 chicken thigh cutlets (1.6kg),
skin removed

2 tablespoons vegetable oil

2 medium brown onions (300g),
sliced thinly

⅓ cup (80ml) lemon juice

¼ cup finely chopped fresh coriander

1 Dry-fry spices and nuts in small heated frying pan, stirring, until nuts are browned lightly.

2 Blend or process nut mixture, ginger and garlic until mixture forms a paste. Combine mixture with yogurt in large bowl, add chicken; mix well. Cover; refrigerate 3 hours or overnight.

3 Heat oil in large saucepan; cook onion, stirring, until soft. Add chicken mixture; simmer, covered, about 45 minutes or until chicken is cooked through. Stir in juice.

4 Serve curry sprinkled with coriander.

__ per serving 64.8g total fat (17.8g saturated fat); 3586kJ (858 cal); 10.4g carbohydrate; 58.1g protein; 3.2g fibre

Called dum ka murgh in India, which immediately indicates the way the chicken is to be cooked: dum cooking slowly steams a dish's ingredients in a tightly sealed pan so that no flavour escapes and very little oil is required. Thought to have been introduced to Indian cooking by the Mughal dynasty from Central Asia, dum is also the name of the casserole dish used, its tight-fitting lid being sealed further with a ring of dough to prevent steam escaping during the cooking process. Today, any good quality pan's lid fits snugly enough to serve this purpose.

preparation time 30 minutes (plus refrigeration time) cooking time 1 hour serves 4

kofta curry

1   Combine mince, ginger, cinnamon, chopped coriander and half the garlic in medium bowl; roll level tablespoons of the mixture into balls. Place balls on tray, cover; refrigerate 30 minutes.
2   Meanwhile, heat one tablespoon of the ghee in large saucepan; cook onion, chilli, spices and remaining garlic, stirring, until onion is browned lightly. Add tomato; cook, stirring, about 5 minutes or until tomato softens. Add stock; simmer, uncovered, about 15 minutes or until sauce thickens slightly.
3   Heat remaining ghee in medium frying pan; cook kofta, in batches, until browned. Add kofta to sauce; simmer, uncovered, about 10 minutes or until kofta are cooked through. Stir in coriander leaves off the heat.
4   Serve kofta curry with a cucumber raita (page 106), if you like.
__ per serving 25.7g total fat (10.8g saturated fat); 1797kJ (430 cal); 6.4g carbohydrate; 42.2g protein; 3.1g fibre

800g chicken mince
2cm piece fresh ginger (10g), grated
½ teaspoon ground cinnamon
⅓ cup coarsely chopped fresh coriander
4 cloves garlic, crushed
2 tablespoons ghee
1 medium brown onion (150g),
  chopped finely
2 fresh long red chillies, chopped finely
2 teaspoons ground coriander
1 teaspoon ground cumin
½ teaspoon ground turmeric
1 teaspoon ground fenugreek
1 teaspoon garam masala (page 112)
4 medium tomatoes (600g), peeled,
  chopped coarsely
2 cups (500ml) chicken stock
½ cup firmly packed fresh coriander leaves

Every culture in the world features some variation of a meatball in its cooking – Danish frikadeller, Mexican albondigas, Italian polpette, Greek keftethes, Croatian cevapcici – but perhaps the name that traverses the widest part of the globe, from the Balkans to North Africa across to India, is kofta (sometimes spelled kefta). This particular version is Pakistani in origin, with a nod to India in its choice of spices. Garam masala is a mixture of assorted aromatic spices used in kitchens throughout the subcontinent. It is available in some supermarkets if you don't have time to make our recipe.

preparation time 35 minutes (plus refrigeration time) cooking time 1 hour serves 4

kenyan chicken curry

8cm piece fresh ginger (40g), grated
6 cloves garlic, crushed
2 teaspoons ground turmeric
½ cup (125ml) lemon juice
⅓ cup (80ml) vegetable oil
1 teaspoon ground cumin
3 teaspoons garam masala (page 112)
1 tablespoon ground coriander
1 teaspoon paprika
1 teaspoon chilli flakes
¼ cup (70g) yogurt
1kg chicken thigh fillets, cut into
    3cm pieces
3 large brown onions (600g),
    chopped coarsely
2 teaspoons chilli powder
2 teaspoons ground fenugreek
2 x 400g cans crushed tomatoes
1 stick cinnamon
2 long green chillies, chopped finely
300ml cream
1 tablespoon honey
¼ cup coarsely chopped fresh coriander

1   Combine half the ginger, half the garlic, half the turmeric, half the juice and half the oil in large bowl with all the cumin, garam masala, ground coriander, paprika, chilli flakes and yogurt, add chicken; turn to coat in marinade. Cover; refrigerate 30 minutes.
2   Preheat oven to very hot (240°C/220°C fan-forced).
3   Cook chicken, in lightly oiled medium shallow flameproof baking dish, uncovered, 10 minutes.
4   Heat remaining oil in large saucepan; cook onion, chilli powder, fenugreek, remaining ginger, garlic and turmeric, stirring, until onion softens. Add undrained tomatoes, cinnamon, green chilli and remaining juice. Simmer, covered, 10 minutes. Stir in cream and honey; simmer, uncovered, 1 minute.
5   Add chicken to curry; simmer about 5 minutes or until chicken is cooked through. Remove from heat, stir in fresh coriander.
__ per serving 58.9g total fat (24g saturated fat); 3035kJ (726 cal); 15.6g carbohydrate; 32.5g protein; 4.9g fibre

Kenyan cooking is a fusion of East African and Middle Eastern methods known by the name of swahili cooking, a word which identifies the culinary influences of traders arriving by sea from the Arabian peninsula upon the indigenous population. This curry uses the pungency of paprika, coriander and turmeric in the chicken marinade to complement the green chilli and fenugreek in the curry.

preparation time 30 minutes (plus refrigeration time) cooking time 30 minutes serves 6

coconut chicken curry

1   Heat oil in large deep flameproof casserole dish; cook chicken, in batches, until browned.
2   Cook ground coriander, crushed garlic, ginger, lemon grass and curry leaves in same pan, stirring, until fragrant.
3   Add onion; cook, stirring, about 5 minutes or until onion softens. Return chicken to pan with cinnamon, cardamom, tamarind, coconut milk and stock; simmer, uncovered, 30 minutes.
4   Add kumara; simmer, uncovered, 30 minutes or until kumara is just tender and chicken is cooked through. Discard cinnamon and cardamom.
5   Meanwhile, combine chopped garlic, chopped ginger, chillies, fresh coriander and rind in small bowl; sprinkle mixture over curry.
__ per serving 61.4g total fat (28.6g saturated fat); 3645kJ (872 cal); 22.8g carbohydrate; 55.8g protein; 5.2g fibre

2 tablespoons vegetable oil
12 chicken drumsticks (1.8kg)
2 tablespoons ground coriander
3 cloves garlic, crushed
5cm piece fresh ginger (25g), grated
10cm stick (20g) fresh lemon grass, chopped finely
10 fresh curry leaves, torn
1 large brown onion (200g), sliced thinly
1 cinnamon stick
2 cardamom pods, bruised
1 tablespoon tamarind concentrate
400g can coconut milk
1 cup (250ml) chicken stock
1 large kumara (500g), chopped coarsely
1 clove garlic, chopped finely
2cm piece fresh ginger (10g), chopped finely
1 fresh small red thai chilli, chopped finely
1 long green chilli, chopped finely
¼ cup finely chopped fresh coriander
2 teaspoons finely grated lemon rind

This curry, also known as opor ayam, is a classic Indonesian dish served mainly on special occasions. A good introduction to diners who are not familiar with the rich, full-flavoured "stews" of South-East Asia, the traditional opor ayam is fragrantly flavourful without being incendiary. Ordinary potato or pumpkin can be used instead of kumara, the orange sweet potato called for here.

preparation time 30 minutes cooking time 1 hour 30 minutes serves 4

beef

Not only is beef a delicious family favourite, it's also an excellent source of health-giving iron. The long simmering times required of the recipes in this chapter are perfect for less expensive cuts of beef, as the slow cooking breaks down the connective tissue, rendering the meat soft, mouth-wateringly tender and infused with aromatic flavour.

trinidadian beef

2 tablespoons coriander seeds
2 tablespoons cumin seeds
½ teaspoon fennel seeds
½ teaspoon black mustard seeds
½ teaspoon fenugreek seeds
1 teaspoon black peppercorns
1 medium brown onion (150g),
  chopped finely
2 cloves garlic, quartered
¼ cup coarsely chopped fresh coriander
1 tablespoon fresh thyme leaves
3 fresh small red thai chillies,
  chopped coarsely
½ teaspoon ground ginger
2 tablespoons coarsely chopped fresh
  flat-leaf parsley
⅓ cup (80ml) peanut oil
1kg gravy beef, cut into 3cm pieces
3 cloves garlic, crushed
1 tablespoon hot curry powder
3 cups (750ml) beef stock
2 fresh small red thai chillies, sliced thinly

1 Dry-fry seeds and peppercorns in small frying pan, stirring, about 1 minute or until fragrant. Crush mixture using mortar and pestle.
2 Blend or process onion, quartered garlic, coriander, thyme, chopped chilli, ginger, parsley and 1 tablespoon of the oil until mixture forms a paste. Transfer curry paste to large bowl; add beef, turn to coat in paste. Cover; refrigerate 30 minutes.
3 Heat remaining oil in large saucepan; cook crushed garlic and curry powder, stirring, 1 minute. Add beef mixture; cook, stirring, over medium heat 10 minutes. Add stock and crushed spice mixture; simmer, covered, 1 hour. Uncover; simmer about 1 hour, stirring occasionally, or until meat is tender and sauce thickens slightly. Serve curry sprinkled with sliced chilli.
__ per serving 30.2g total fat (8.3g saturated fat); 2111kJ (505 cal); 3.7g carbohydrate; 53.9g protein; 1.9g fibre

The food of Trinidad (an island located in the southeast Caribbean off the coast of Venezuela) was developed by the influence of East Indian and African cultures, whose people had been brought in to work in the local plantations as slaves. It is identified by its deep, rich spicing, rather than any excessive heat from chillies.
Thyme is a member of the mint family, it has tiny grey-green leaves that give off a pungent minty, light-lemon aroma.

preparation time 25 minutes (plus refrigeration time) cooking time 2 hours 15 minutes serves 4

braised oxtail
in peanut sauce

1 Coat oxtail in flour; shake off excess. Heat half the oil in large flameproof casserole dish; cook oxtail, in batches, until browned.
2 Heat remaining oil in same dish; cook onion and garlic, stirring, until onion softens. Add spices and chilli; cook, stirring, until fragrant. Return oxtail to dish with stock and the water; simmer, covered, 2 hours.
3 Strain beef over large bowl; reserve braising liquid, discard solids. Skim fat from braising liquid.
4 Cook curry paste in same cleaned dish, stirring, until fragrant. Add 4 cups of the reserved braising liquid; bring to a boil. Add oxtail; simmer, uncovered, about 45 minutes or until oxtail is tender.
5 Add nuts and beans to dish; cook, uncovered, about 5 minutes or until beans are tender.
6 Serve curry sprinkled with green onion.

__ per serving 111.7g total fat (36.8g saturated fat); 5626kJ (1346 cal); 15.6g carbohydrate; 70g protein; 6.7 g fibre

2 oxtails (2kg), cut into 5cm pieces
2 tablespoons plain flour
2 tablespoons vegetable oil
1 large brown onion (200g),
  chopped coarsely
6 cloves garlic, crushed
1 tablespoon ground coriander
1 tablespoon ground cumin
2 star anise
2 fresh long red chillies, halved lengthways
1 litre (4 cups) beef stock
1 litre (4 cups) water
⅔ cup (200g) red curry paste (page 110)
⅔ cup (90g) roasted unsalted peanuts,
  chopped coarsely
300g green beans, trimmed,
  chopped coarsely
2 green onions, sliced thinly

While originally oxtail was just what it sounds like, meat from the tail of an ox, these days it's more likely to be from any beef cattle. A flavourful cut, it is also fatty so, to reduce the fat count dramatically, make the recipe through to step 3, refrigerate it overnight, then skim away the solidified fat on the surface before continuing making the curry. This recipe is a variation of a Philippine curry, kare-kare, which sometimes includes tripe and various in-season vegetables, and is generally served at fiestas.

preparation time 30 minutes cooking time 3 hours 20 minutes serves 4

thai red beef curry

1 tablespoon peanut oil
4 x 125g scotch fillet steaks
¼ cup (75g) red curry paste (page 110)
225g can bamboo shoots, drained, rinsed
2 x 400ml cans coconut cream
½ cup (125ml) beef stock
2 tablespoons fish sauce
2 tablespoons lime juice
2 fresh kaffir lime leaves, shredded finely
4 large zucchini (600g), sliced thinly
⅓ cup firmly packed fresh thai basil leaves

1   Heat oil in large flameproof casserole dish; cook beef, in batches, until well-browned both sides.
2   Cook paste in same dish, stirring, until fragrant. Return beef to dish with bamboo shoots, coconut cream, stock, sauce, juice and lime leaves; simmer, uncovered, 1 hour 20 minutes. Add zucchini, simmer about 5 minutes or until tender.
3   Serve curry sprinkled with basil.
TIP   Add one or two finely chopped fresh red chillies along with the bamboo shoots for extra heat, if desired.
__ per serving 55.5g total fat (40.6g saturated fat); 2897kJ (693 cal); 12.3g carbohydrate; 34.1g protein; 7.2g fibre

South-East Asian food, in general, is far more complex than our own, having four distinct tastes – sweet, salty, spicy, sour – and a less dominant fifth, bitter. Nowhere do these different flavours meet and blend more harmoniously than in Thai curries such as this one, a perfect amalgam of sweet (coconut cream), salty (fish sauce), spicy (thai red curry paste) and sour (kaffir lime). Only a homemade curry paste can fully impart the subtleties of these taste sensations to a finished dish, and what you don't use of our red curry paste recipe here can be covered tightly and frozen for future use.
Bamboo shoots, the tender shoots of bamboo plants, are available in cans, and must be drained and rinsed before use.

preparation time 15 minutes cooking time 1 hour 40 minutes serves 4

massaman curry

1   Place beef, 1½ cups of the stock, cardamom, clove, star anise, sugar, sauce, 1 tablespoon of the tamarind and half of the coconut milk in large saucepan; simmer, uncovered, about 1½ hours or until beef is almost tender.

2   Strain beef over large bowl; reserve braising liquid, discard solids. Cover beef to keep warm.

3   Cook curry paste in same pan, stirring, until fragrant. Add remaining coconut milk, tamarind and stock; bring to a boil. Cook, stirring, about 1 minute or until mixture is smooth. Return beef to pan with brown onion, kumara and 1 cup of the reserved braising liquid; simmer, uncovered, about 30 minutes or until beef and vegetables are tender.

4   Stir nuts and green onion into curry off the heat.

__ per serving 52.7g total fat (39.5g saturated fat); 3645kJ (872 cal); 29.2g carbohydrate; 67.4g protein; 7.2g fibre

1kg skirt steak, cut into 3cm pieces
2 cups (500ml) beef stock
5 cardamom pods, bruised
¼ teaspoon ground clove
2 star anise
1 tablespoon grated palm sugar
2 tablespoons fish sauce
2 tablespoons tamarind concentrate
2 x 400ml cans coconut milk
2 tablespoons massaman curry paste
  (page 113)
8 baby brown onions (200g), halved
1 medium kumara (400g), chopped coarsely
¼ cup (35g) coarsely chopped roasted
  unsalted peanuts
2 green onions, sliced thinly

Using spices carried to Thailand by Muslim traders from the West, this richly flavoured curry has the fragrant aroma and taste of many Middle Eastern dishes. It is one of the staples found on dining tables in the Muslim communities located mainly in the south of Thailand close to the Malaysian border.

preparation time 20 minutes cooking time 2 hours 10 minutes serves 4

xacutti

1 cup (80g) desiccated coconut
½ teaspoon ground cinnamon
4 whole cloves
8 dried long red chillies
1 teaspoon ground turmeric
1 tablespoon poppy seeds
1 tablespoon cumin seeds
1 tablespoon fennel seeds
2 tablespoons coriander seeds
2 teaspoons black peppercorns
2 star anise
6 cloves garlic, quartered
2 tablespoons ghee
1 large brown onion (200g), chopped finely
1kg diced rump
2 cups (500ml) water
2 cups (500ml) beef stock
2 tablespoons lime juice

1 Dry-fry coconut in large frying pan over medium heat, stirring, until browned lightly; remove coconut from pan. Dry-fry cinnamon, cloves, chillies, turmeric, seeds, peppercorns and star anise in same pan, stirring, about 1 minute or until fragrant.
2 Blend or process coconut, spice mixture and garlic until fine.
3 Heat ghee in large saucepan; cook onion, stirring, until onion softens. Add coconut spice mixture; cook, stirring, until fragrant. Add beef; cook, stirring, about 2 minutes or until beef is coated with coconut spice mixture.
4 Add the water and stock; simmer, covered, 30 minutes, stirring occasionally. Uncover; cook 30 minutes or until beef is tender and sauce thickened slightly. Stir juice into curry off the heat; sprinkle with fresh sliced chilli if you like.
__ per serving 38.2g total fat (23.8g saturated fat); 2512kJ (600 cal); 5g carbohydrate; 57.5g protein; 5.2g fibre

Xacutti (pronounced sha-koo-tee) is a Goan curry, perhaps not as well known as the vindaloo, another speciality of the formerly Portuguese, now Indian, state. Traditionally made with mutton or chicken and a dry curry paste containing fried coconut, it has lime juice added just before serving, which further distinguishes it from a vinegary vindaloo.

preparation time 25 minutes cooking time 1 hour 15 minutes serves 4

aromatic vietnamese
beef curry

1   Heat half of the oil in wok; stir-fry beef, in batches, until browned. Cover to keep warm.

2   Heat remaining oil in same wok; stir-fry onion until soft. Add garlic, chilli, lemon grass, star anise, cinnamon, cardamom and beans; stir-fry until beans are tender. Discard star anise, cinnamon and cardamom. Return beef to wok with sauces; stir-fry until heated through. Stir in coriander and nuts off the heat.

__ per serving 27.2g total fat (7.1g saturated fat); 2011kJ (481 cal); 7.4g carbohydrate; 49.6g protein; 4.9g fibre

2 tablespoons peanut oil

800g beef strips

1 medium brown onion (150g), chopped finely

3 cloves garlic, crushed

1 fresh long red chilli, chopped finely

10cm stick (20g) fresh lemon grass, chopped finely

1 star anise

1 cinnamon stick

4 cardamom pods, bruised

350g snake beans, cut in 4cm lengths

2 tablespoons ground bean sauce

2 tablespoons fish sauce

½ cup coarsely chopped fresh coriander

½ cup (40g) toasted almond flakes

Modern Vietnamese cuisine reflects the influence of the country's previous French colonists, whereas the traditional food of the people has more in common with neighbouring Chinese dishes. One distinguishing note, however, is that the Vietnamese use fish sauce extensively while Chinese cooking relies more on the presence of soy sauce.

preparation time 15 minutes cooking time 20 minutes serves 4

meatballs in spicy coconut milk

800g beef mince

2 eggs

2 teaspoons cornflour

2 cloves garlic, crushed

1 tablespoon finely chopped
  fresh coriander

1 fresh long red chilli, chopped finely

2 purple shallots (50g), chopped coarsely

3 cloves garlic, quartered

1 teaspoon chilli flakes

7 fresh long red chillies, chopped coarsely

2 tablespoons peanut oil

2cm piece fresh galangal (10g), sliced thinly

3 large tomatoes (660g), seeded,
  chopped coarsely

400ml can coconut milk

1 tablespoon kecap asin

1 large tomato (220g), seeded, diced

½ cup (40g) fried shallots

1 fresh small red chilli, sliced thinly

1   Combine mince, eggs, cornflour, crushed garlic, coriander and finely chopped chilli in medium bowl; roll level tablespoons of mixture into balls. Place meatballs, in single layer, in large baking-paper-lined bamboo steamer. Steam, covered, over wok of simmering water 10 minutes.

2   Meanwhile, blend or process purple shallots, quartered garlic, chilli flakes, coarsely chopped chilli and half of the oil until mixture forms a paste.

3   Heat remaining oil in wok; cook shallot paste and galangal, stirring, about 1 minute or until fragrant. Add chopped tomato; cook, stirring, 1 minute. Add coconut milk, kecap asin and meatballs; simmer, uncovered, stirring occasionally, about 5 minutes or until meatballs are cooked through and sauce thickens slightly.

4   Serve curry topped with diced tomato, fried shallots and thinly sliced chilli.

__ per serving 47.1g total fat (26.5g saturated fat); 2721kJ (651 cal); 8.3g carbohydrate; 47.7g protein; 3.9g fibre

This recipe showcases the significant influences on Singaporean cooking taken from the cuisines of its near neighbours. Borrowing culinary techniques from Malaysia, India and China, chillies and spices laced with coconut milk are a characteristic of this island nation's cuisine. Kecap asin, an astringent, salty soy sauce native to the cooking of Indonesia, is available from Asian food stores.

preparation time 25 minutes cooking time 20 minutes serves 4

beef do-piaza

1   Combine yogurt and saffron in small bowl. Set aside.
2   Heat vegetable oil in large flameproof casserole dish;
cook beef, in batches, until browned all over.
3   Cook chopped onion in same dish, stirring, until soft. Add
spices, garlic, ginger and chilli; cook, stirring, until fragrant.
Add undrained tomatoes and stock; bring to a boil. Return
beef to dish; simmer, covered, about 1½ hours or until beef
is tender. Stir in yogurt mixture.
4   Meanwhile, heat peanut oil in large frying pan; cook sliced
onion, stirring, until browned lightly. Sprinkle over curry to serve.
—— per serving 36.6g total fat (9.3g saturated fat); 2617kJ
(626 cal); 14.8g carbohydrate; 57.5g protein; 4.7g fibre

200g yogurt
¼ teaspoon saffron threads
¼ cup (60ml) vegetable oil
1kg chuck steak, cut into 2cm pieces
2 medium brown onions (300g),
   chopped finely
2 teaspoons ground cumin
2 teaspoons coriander seeds
1 teaspoon ground cardamom
1 teaspoon ground fenugreek
½ teaspoon ground turmeric
2 cloves garlic, crushed
2cm piece fresh ginger (10g), grated
2 long green chillies, sliced thinly
2 x 400g cans crushed tomatoes
1 cup (250ml) beef stock
2 tablespoons peanut oil
2 medium brown onions (300g),
   sliced thinly

Do-piaza, meaning "two-onions",
is a dish from the Hydrabad
region of India and does not
refer to the amount of onions
used in the recipe but to the way
they are separately treated. In
this recipe, one onion is chopped
finely and one is sliced thinly,
giving the dish a unique texture.

preparation time 30 minutes cooking time 2 hours serves 4

lamb

Unlike pork or beef, lamb is used for curries in every nation that makes them as part of their everyday range of dishes. In part, this is due to religious tradition, but mainly because the distinct sweet flavour of lamb blends so well with the various fragrant, astringent or spicy ingredients used in a typical curry.

rogan josh

1 tablespoon vegetable oil

1kg lamb shoulder, diced into 3cm pieces

3 medium brown onions (450g), sliced thinly

4cm piece fresh ginger (20g), grated

2 cloves garlic, crushed

⅔ cup (200g) prepared rogan josh paste

1½ cups (375ml) water

425g can diced tomatoes

1 cinnamon stick

5 cardamom pods, bruised

2 tablespoons coarsely chopped fresh coriander

1 Heat half the oil in large saucepan; cook lamb, in batches, until browned.

2 Heat remaining oil in same pan; cook onion, stirring, until soft. Add ginger, garlic and paste; cook, stirring, until fragrant.

3 Return lamb to pan; stir to combine with paste mixture. Add the water, undrained tomatoes, cinnamon and cardamom; simmer, covered, about 1½ hours or until lamb is tender. Serve curry sprinkled with coriander.

__ per serving 28.6g total fat (8.3g saturated fat); 1835kJ (439 cal); 7.8g carbohydrate; 35.7g protein; 5.5g fibre

Rogan josh, traditionally made with lamb, is an Indian tomato-based curry, and literally means "meat in spicy red sauce". It is slightly milder than many curries due in equal part to the fairly large amount of tomato used and the very little chilli found in the paste.

preparation time 25 minutes cooking time 1 hour 50 minutes serves 6

lamb stoba

1   Heat half the oil in large saucepan; cook lamb, in batches, until browned all over.
2   Heat remaining oil in same pan; cook onion, ginger, chilli, capsicum and spices, stirring, until onion softens.
3   Add lamb and remaining ingredients; simmer, covered, about 1 hour or until lamb is tender.
__ per serving 31.8g total fat (11.2g saturated fat); 2567kJ (614 cal); 24.4g carbohydrate; 55.8g protein; 4.1g fibre

2 tablespoons vegetable oil
1kg lamb shoulder, trimmed, diced
   into 3cm pieces
2 medium brown onions (300g),
   sliced thinly
3cm piece fresh ginger (15g), sliced thinly
2 fresh long red chillies, sliced thinly
1 medium red capsicum (200g),
   chopped coarsely
2 teaspoons ground cumin
2 teaspoons ground allspice
1 cinnamon stick
2 x 400g cans chopped tomatoes
2 teaspoons finely grated lime rind
2 tablespoons lime juice
¼ cup (55g) firmly packed brown sugar

Stoba, a popular stew eaten throughout the islands of the Caribbean, is usually made with goat, but we've used lamb because it's easier to find. If you can get goat, however, do try this recipe using a kilo of any trimmed cubed cut of meat.

preparation time 10 minutes cooking time 1 hour 30 minutes serves 4

afghani lamb and spinach curry

1½ tablespoons vegetable oil
1kg lamb shoulder, trimmed, diced into
 3cm pieces
1 large brown onion (200g), chopped finely
4 cloves garlic, crushed
2 teaspoons ground turmeric
½ teaspoon ground nutmeg
½ teaspoon ground cinnamon
½ teaspoon cayenne pepper
400g can chopped tomatoes
2 cups (500ml) beef stock
350g spinach
1 tablespoon finely grated lemon rind
⅓ cup (45g) toasted slivered almonds

1 Heat half the oil in large saucepan; cook lamb, in batches, until browned all over.
2 Heat remaining oil in same pan; cook onion, garlic and spices, stirring, until onion softens.
3 Add lamb, undrained tomatoes and stock; simmer, covered, about 1 hour. Uncover; simmer 15 minutes or until sauce thickens and lamb is tender. Add spinach and rind; stir over heat about 1 minute or until spinach wilts. Serve curry sprinkled with almonds.
— per serving 36g total fat (11.4g saturated fat); 2516kJ (602 cal); 7.2g carbohydrate; 60g protein; 5.9g fibre

Sandwiched between the Middle East and the Indian subcontinent, Afghanistan food has been influenced by the cuisines of all the countries in these areas. In this recipe, its Iranian and Turkish influences are shown by the addition of nutmeg and cinnamon, while the rich, thick sauce from the combined tomato, stock and spinach resemble a traditional Indian curry. The tender green leaves of spinach are often added to soups, stir-fries and curries just before serving.

preparation time 20 minutes cooking time 1 hour 30 minutes serves 4

keema with green chilli and tomato

1 Heat ghee in large saucepan; cook onion, ginger, garlic and two-thirds of the chilli, stirring, until onion softens. Add spices; cook, stirring, until fragrant. Add mince; cook, stirring, until mince changes colour.

2 Add undrained tomatoes and fresh tomato; cook, stirring occasionally, about 15 minutes or until mince is cooked through and sauce has thickened.

3 Add remaining chilli, yogurt, juice and peas; cook, uncovered, until peas are just tender. Serve curry sprinkled with coriander.

__ per serving 4.6g total fat (2.4g saturated fat); 364kJ (87 cal); 2.2g carbohydrate; 8.8g protein; 1.2g fibre

2 tablespoons ghee
1 medium brown onion (150g), chopped finely
5cm piece fresh ginger (25g), grated
2 cloves garlic, crushed
3 long green chillies, chopped finely
2 teaspoons cumin seeds
2 teaspoons ground coriander
1 teaspoon ground turmeric
2 teaspoons garam masala (page 112)
800g lamb mince
400g can diced tomatoes
2 large tomatoes (440g), chopped coarsely
⅓ cup (95g) yogurt
1 tablespoon lemon juice
1 cup (120g) frozen peas
2 tablespoons coarsely chopped fresh coriander

Keema is minced meat, usually beef or lamb, and is the meat found in samosas. Here, our subtle, yet fragrant, curry is fairly dry, not unlike a bolognese sauce, and can be eaten in the hand, picked up by pieces of roti or naan. Cooked down further, it can be treated as a filling for "pan rolls", an Indian version of a crépe that, once stuffed, is crumbed and shallow-fried.

preparation time 20 minutes cooking time 45 minutes serves 4

nepalese meatball curry

2 tablespoons vegetable oil
1 small white onion (80g), chopped finely
3 cloves garlic, crushed
5cm piece fresh ginger (25g), grated
750g lamb mince
1 egg
1 egg yolk
1 fresh long red chilli, chopped finely
1 teaspoon ground cumin
½ teaspoon ground turmeric
¼ cup coarsely chopped fresh coriander
2 tablespoons stale breadcrumbs
¼ cup (60ml) lemon juice
CURRY SAUCE
1 tablespoon vegetable oil
1 medium white onion (150g),
  chopped finely
1 clove garlic, crushed
3cm piece fresh ginger (15g), grated
1 tablespoon coarsely chopped coriander
  root and stem mixture
2 teaspoons ground cumin
1 teaspoon ground fenugreek
1 teaspoon yellow mustard seeds
1 teaspoon ground turmeric
2 x 400g cans crushed tomatoes
1 cup (250ml) beef stock

1 Make curry sauce.
2 Meanwhile, heat half of the oil in large frying pan; cook onion, garlic and ginger, stirring, until onion softens. Cool 10 minutes.
3 Combine mince, whole egg and yolk, chilli, spices, coriander, breadcrumbs and onion mixture in large bowl; roll level tablespoons of the lamb mixture into balls.
4 Heat remaining oil in same pan; cook meatballs, in batches, until browned all over.
5 Add meatballs to curry sauce; cook, uncovered, about 20 minutes or until meatballs are cooked through. Stir juice into curry off the heat.
CURRY SAUCE Heat oil in large saucepan; cook onion, garlic and ginger, stirring, until onion softens. Add coriander mixture and spices; cook, stirring, until fragrant. Add undrained tomatoes and stock; simmer, covered, 1 hour.
__ per serving 29.9g total fat (8.4g saturated fat); 2086kJ (499 cal); 12.2g carbohydrate; 43.7g protein; 4.1g fibre

preparation time 30 minutes **cooking time** 1 hour 20 minutes **serves** 4

Nepalese food, heavily influenced by the neighbouring countries of India and Tibet, uses mostly lamb in its cooking because, like its neighbour to the south, the country's predominant religion is Hindu, which holds the cow sacred.

lamb korma

1 Blend or process nuts until finely ground.

2 Heat 2 tablespoons of the ghee in large saucepan; cook lamb, in batches, until browned.

3 Heat remaining ghee in same pan; cook onion, garlic and ginger, stirring, until onion softens. Add ground nuts, seeds and paste; cook, stirring, until fragrant.

4 Return lamb to pan with stock and cream; simmer, uncovered, about 15 minutes or until sauce thickens slightly. Serve korma accompanied by yogurt.

— per serving 84.1g total fat (40.3g saturated fat); 4172kJ (998 cal); 9.2g carbohydrate; 50.6g protein; 6.4g fibre

⅓ cup (55g) blanched almonds
3 tablespoons ghee
800g lamb strips
1 large brown onion (200g), sliced thinly
2 cloves garlic, crushed
4cm piece fresh ginger (20g), grated
2 teaspoons poppy seeds
½ cup (150g) prepared korma paste
½ cup (125ml) chicken stock
300ml cream
⅓ cup (95g) yogurt

Lamb korma is a fairly mild, rich curry, its sauce pale with cream and its flavour enhanced by the delicate use of nutmeg, saffron and cardamom. This recipe uses a pre made paste, which is easily found in supermarkets.

preparation time 25 minutes (plus refrigeration time) cooking time 40 minutes serves 4

lamb rendang

2 teaspoons coriander seeds
¼ teaspoon ground turmeric
2 large brown onions (400g),
   chopped coarsely
4 cloves garlic, quartered
2 x 10cm sticks (40g) fresh lemon grass,
   chopped coarsely
2cm piece fresh galangal (10g), sliced thinly
4 fresh small red thai chillies,
   chopped coarsely
2 fresh long red chillies, chopped coarsely
2 tablespoons coarsely chopped coriander
   root and stem mixture
2 tablespoons peanut oil
1.5kg butterflied leg of lamb
400ml can coconut milk

1   Dry-fry spices in small frying pan, stirring, about 1 minute or until fragrant. Blend or process spices with onion, garlic, lemon grass, galangal, chillies and coriander mixture until mixture forms a paste.
2   Preheat oven to slow (150°C/130°C fan-forced).
3   Heat half of the oil in large flameproof baking dish; cook lamb, turning occasionally, until browned all over. Remove from dish.
4   Heat remaining oil in same dish; cook onion paste, stirring, until fragrant. Add coconut milk; bring to a boil.
5   Return lamb to dish; cook in oven, uncovered, turning occasionally, about 3 hours or until liquid has evaporated. Cover lamb; stand 10 minutes before serving.
__ per serving 50.2g total fat (28.8g saturated fat); 3490kJ (835 cal); 8.1g carbohydrate; 86.5g protein; 3.7g fibre

We've given a spin to a classic rendang, the Malaysian meat curry that is also eaten throughout Indonesia and in Singapore. Traditionally slowly cooked until the coconut milk sauce thickens and is quite dry, the succulent meat becomes so tender it virtually falls apart.

preparation time 30 minutes **cooking time** 3 hours 15 minutes **serves** 4

malaysian lamb curry

1 Combine spices in large bowl, add lamb; mix well.

2 Heat two tablespoons of the oil in large saucepan; cook lamb mixture, in batches, until browned.

3 Heat remaining oil in same pan; cook onion, garlic and chillies over low heat, stirring, until onion softens.

4 Return lamb to pan with coconut cream and stock; simmer, covered, 1 hour 20 minutes. Uncover, stir in peas off the heat. Serve curry sprinkled with coriander.

— per serving 57.4g total fat (30g saturated fat); 3390kJ (811 cal); 12.3g carbohydrate; 58.4g protein; 8.5g fibre

2 tablespoons garam masala (page 112)
1 tablespoon ground cumin
1 tablespoon black mustard seeds
1 teaspoon ground turmeric
1kg diced lamb shoulder
¼ cup (60ml) vegetable oil
2 medium brown onions (300g), sliced thinly
2 cloves garlic, crushed
3 dried long red chillies, chopped coarsely
2 long green chillies, chopped coarsely
400ml can coconut cream
1 cup (250ml) beef stock
200g sugar snap peas, trimmed
½ cup loosely packed fresh coriander leaves

This rich combination of spices cooked in coconut cream is classic Malaysian cooking, combining the country's Indian and Straits Chinese influences. This recipe uses black mustard seeds (sometimes sold as brown mustard seeds), which are more pungent than the white (or yellow) seeds used in most prepared mustards.

preparation time 20 minutes cooking time 1 hour 30 minutes serves 4

pork

While some cultures don't eat much, if any, pork, the fact remains that it is perfect for currying. The distinctively rich, full taste of this "other white meat" lends itself to being matched with equally strong, robust flavours, particularly those common to the food of South-East Asia such as tamarind, vinegar, coriander, fish sauce and lemon grass.

sour pork curry

1 tablespoon vegetable oil

1kg pork neck

1 teaspoon shrimp paste

¼ cup coarsely chopped coriander
root and stem mixture

2cm piece fresh galangal (10g),
chopped finely

5 dried long red chillies, chopped finely

3 fresh long red chillies, chopped finely

2 tablespoons fish sauce

¾ cup (235g) tamarind concentrate

2 tablespoons caster sugar

2 cups (500ml) chicken stock

1 litre (4 cups) water

½ cup fresh thai basil leaves,
chopped coarsely

1   Heat oil in large flameproof casserole dish; cook pork, uncovered, until browned. Remove from dish.

2   Preheat oven to moderately slow (170°C/150°C fan-forced).

3   Add paste, coriander mixture, galangal and chillies to same dish; cook, stirring, until fragrant. Add sauce, tamarind, sugar, stock and the water; bring to a boil. Return pork to dish, cover; cook in oven 1 hour. Uncover; cook 1 hour.

4   Remove pork from dish, cover; stand 10 minutes before slicing thickly. Stir basil into curry sauce off the heat.

__ per serving 9.3g total fat (2.1g saturated fat); 1680kJ (402 cal); 18.3g carbohydrate; 59.7g protein; 1.5g fibre

Sour curries, simple to make but slow cooking, are considered street food in Bangkok, where they're served with pickles and steamed rice. Street vendors make inexpensive food readily available to busy workers and also provide a colourful source of the smells and tastes of this unique city's culture.
Thai basil, also known as horapa, is available from greengrocers and Asian supermarkets.

preparation time 30 minutes cooking time 2 hours 15 minutes serves 4

pork and lemon grass curry

1   Blend or process lemon grass, garlic, galangal, turmeric and chilli with the water until mixture forms a paste.

2   Heat 1 tablespoon of the oil in large saucepan; cook lemon grass paste and shrimp paste, stirring, about 1 minute or until fragrant. Add coconut milk and lime leaves; simmer, uncovered, about 30 minutes or until sauce thickens slightly.

3   Meanwhile, heat remaining oil in large frying pan. Cook pork, in batches, until browned. Add pork and juice to curry sauce; simmer, uncovered, about 2 minutes or until pork is cooked.

__ per serving 75.2g total fat (45.6g saturated fat); 3925kJ (939 cal); 8.3g carbohydrate; 57.3g protein; 4.2g fibre

3 x 10cm sticks (60g) fresh lemon grass, chopped finely
4 cloves garlic, quartered
4cm piece (20g) fresh galangal, sliced thinly
1 teaspoon ground turmeric
2 fresh jalapeño chillies, quartered
½ cup (125ml) water
¼ cup (60ml) peanut oil
½ teaspoon shrimp paste
2 x 400ml cans coconut milk
3 fresh kaffir lime leaves, torn
1kg pork fillet, cut into 1cm slices
2 tablespoons lime juice

This curry is of Cambodian origin, a country whose cuisine uses some of the flavours from two of its near-neighbours, Thailand and Vietnam, but is somewhat simpler and more refined. A close relative of ginger, galangal is an important ingredient in the foods of South-East Asia and is commonly called for in recipes. The flavour is stronger and more intense than that of ginger, so use it sparingly or to your taste.

preparation time 20 minutes cooking time 45 minutes serves 4

nepalese pork mince curry

2 tablespoons peanut oil
2 tablespoons yellow mustard seeds
2 teaspoons ground cumin
1 teaspoon ground turmeric
2 teaspoons garam masala (page 112)
3 cloves garlic, crushed
4cm piece fresh ginger (20g), grated
2 medium brown onions (300g),
  chopped finely
800g pork mince
½ cup (125ml) water
¼ cup coarsely chopped fresh coriander

1 Heat oil in large frying pan; cook seeds, stirring, about 2 minutes or until seeds pop. Add cumin, turmeric and garam masala; cook, stirring, 2 minutes.
2 Add garlic, ginger and onion; cook, stirring, until onion softens.
3 Add mince; cook, stirring, until cooked through. Add the water; simmer, uncovered, 15 minutes. Remove from heat, stir in coriander.
__ per serving 23.4g total fat (6.9g saturated fat); 1655kJ (396 cal); 4g carbohydrate; 41.4g protein; 2.6g fibre

This dry, fragrant Nepalese curry, made with pork mince and usually served with steamed rice and lime wedges, is one of this small Himalayan country's most popular meat dishes. Another is the delectable momo, a delicate steamed or pan-fried meat-filled dumpling eaten by the cold-climate mountain-dwelling people of both Nepal and Tibet.

preparation time 15 minutes cooking time 20 minutes serves 4

tamarind and citrus pork curry

1   Soak tamarind in the boiling water 30 minutes. Place fine sieve over small bowl; push tamarind through sieve. Discard solids in sieve; reserve pulp in bowl.
2   Heat oil in large saucepan; cook onion, chilli, ginger, garlic, curry leaves, seeds and spices, stirring, until onion softens.
3   Add pulp, rind, juice, coconut cream and eggplant; simmer, covered, 20 minutes. Add pork; simmer, uncovered, about 20 minutes or until pork is cooked.

__ per serving 45.8g total fat (25.7g saturated fat); 3060kJ (732 cal); 19.7g carbohydrate; 57.7g protein; 6.8g fibre

70g dried tamarind, chopped coarsely
¾ cup (180ml) boiling water
1 tablespoon peanut oil
1 large red onion (300g), chopped finely
1 fresh long red chilli, sliced thinly
5cm piece fresh ginger (25g), grated
2 cloves garlic, crushed
10 fresh curry leaves
2 teaspoons fenugreek seeds
½ teaspoon ground turmeric
1 teaspoon ground coriander
1 teaspoon finely grated lime rind
1 tablespoon lime juice
400ml can coconut cream
6 baby eggplants (360g), chopped coarsely
1kg pork fillet, cut into 2cm dice

Cambodian food uses techniques and ingredients from Chinese, Indian and Thai cooking, but distils them into an individual style. This recipe smacks of Indian influence, but it's individualised with native ingredients and flavours such as tamarind, the tangy-tasting dried pod of the tamarind tree.

preparation time 20 minutes (plus standing time) cooking time 50 minutes serves 4

pork vindaloo

2 tablespoons ghee
1kg pork shoulder, cut into 3cm pieces
1 large red onion (300g), sliced thinly
½ cup (150g) prepared vindaloo paste
2 cloves garlic, crushed
2 cups (500ml) water
¼ cup (60ml) white vinegar
4 medium potatoes (800g), quartered
2 fresh small red thai chillies, chopped finely
2 fresh long red chillies, sliced thinly

1   Heat ghee in large saucepan; cook pork, in batches, until browned all over.
2   Cook onion in same pan, stirring, until soft. Add paste and garlic; cook, stirring, about 1 minute or until fragrant.
3   Return pork to pan with the water and vinegar; simmer, covered, 50 minutes.
4   Add potato; simmer, uncovered, about 45 minutes or until potato is tender. Stir in chopped chilli; serve curry sprinkled with thinly sliced chilli.
__ per serving 40.7g total fat (13.7g saturated fat); 3173kJ (759 cal); 33.3g carbohydrate; 61g protein; 8.3g fibre

The king of curries, the fiery Indian vindaloo, is from the former Portuguese colony of Goa. The name is derived from the Portuguese words for vinegar and garlic, the dish's primary ingredients. Jars of vindaloo paste are available in supermarkets.

preparation time 25 minutes cooking time 1 hour 50 minutes serves 4

sri lankan fried pork curry

1   Heat half the oil in large saucepan; cook leaves and seeds until seeds pop and mixture is fragrant. Add onion, garlic and ginger; cook, stirring, until onion softens.

2   Add curry powder and cayenne to pan, then pork; stir well to combine. Add vinegar, tamarind, cinnamon, cardamom and the water; simmer, covered, 1 hour.

3   Heat remaining oil in large frying pan. Transfer pork to pan; cook, stirring, until pork is browned and crisp.

4   Meanwhile, add coconut milk to curry sauce; simmer, stirring, about 5 minutes or until curry thickens slightly. Return pork to curry; stir to combine.

__ per serving 78.2g total fat (35.7g saturated fat); 3766kJ (901 cal); 8g carbohydrate; 42.1g protein; 3.6g fibre

2 tablespoons vegetable oil
20 fresh curry leaves
½ teaspoon fenugreek seeds
1 large brown onion (200g), chopped finely
4 cloves garlic, crushed
3cm piece fresh ginger (15g), grated
1 tablespoon curry powder
2 teaspoons cayenne pepper
1kg pork belly, chopped coarsely
1 tablespoon white wine vinegar
2 tablespoons tamarind concentrate
1 cinnamon stick
4 cardamom pods, bruised
1½ cups (375ml) water
400ml can coconut milk

Sri Lanka, that small island situated at the southernmost tip of India, was occupied by a large number of different cultures in the past, and it is probably due to the Dutch and English that pork remains one of its most consumed meats. This curry is typically cooked with the fat left on, to give the dish a deep richness of flavour, which is tempered by the astringency of the vinegar and tamarind.

preparation time 20 minutes cooking time 1 hour 20 minutes serves 4

vegetarian

Vegetables are not only good for you because they're loaded with vitamins and minerals (with only a very few containing any fat), they're at their most scrumptious when used as the main ingredient in a curry. These recipes make use of a wide range of vegetables, and each one is better than the next.

palak paneer

1 tablespoon vegetable oil
1 teaspoon cumin seeds
1 teaspoon fenugreek seeds
2 teaspoons garam masala (page 112)
1 large brown onion (200g), chopped finely
1 clove garlic, crushed
1 tablespoon lemon juice
500g spinach, trimmed, chopped coarsely
¾ cup (180ml) cream
2 x 100g packets paneer cheese, cut
   into 2cm pieces

1   Heat oil in large frying pan; cook spices, onion and garlic, stirring, until onion softens.
2   Add juice and half of the spinach; cook, stirring, until spinach wilts. Add remaining spinach; cook, stirring, until wilted.
3   Blend or process spinach mixture until smooth; return to pan; stir in cream. Add paneer; cook over low heat, uncovered, stirring occasionally, about 5 minutes or until heated through.
__ per serving 24.2g total fat (14.1g saturated fat); 1124kJ (269 cal); 3g carbohydrate; 9g protein; 3.4g fibre

This luscious spinach and cheese dish comes from northern India, the home of paneer, a fresh cow-milk cheese similar to ricotta. It's sold near the fetta and haloumi in supermarkets; either of these two cheeses can replace paneer here, but the results won't be exactly the same.

preparation time 10 minutes cooking time 20 minutes serves 6

okra and tomato in coconut sauce

1   Blend or process garlic, shallot, chilli, onion and tamarind until smooth.

2   Heat oil in large saucepan; add tamarind mixture. Cook, stirring, 2 minutes. Add coconut milk, juice and curry leaves; simmer, uncovered 5 minutes.

3   Add okra and undrained tomatoes; simmer, uncovered, about 20 minutes or until okra is tender.

__ per serving 29.5g total fat (18.8g saturated fat); 1384kJ (331 cal); 13.4g carbohydrate; 7.6g protein; 8.9g fibre

5 cloves garlic, quartered
3 shallots (75g), chopped coarsely
2 fresh long red chillies, chopped coarsely
2 green onions, chopped finely
⅓ cup (100g) tamarind concentrate
1 tablespoon vegetable oil
400g can coconut milk
2 tablespoons lime juice
10 fresh curry leaves
500g fresh okra, halved lengthways
400g can crushed tomatoes

Okra, also called bamia, bhindi or ladies fingers, are an African vegetable transported throughout the world by African slaves and traders. Okra resembles a large green chilli having outside ribs and many edible, gummy seeds inside. It can be stewed, as here, roasted or deep-fried, and is as good eaten on its own as it is used in stews, casseroles and soups.

preparation time 15 minutes cooking time 30 minutes serves 4

chickpeas in spicy tomato sauce

2 tablespoons ghee
2 teaspoons cumin seeds
2 medium brown onions (300g),
  chopped finely
2 cloves garlic, crushed
4cm piece fresh ginger (20g), grated
1 tablespoon ground coriander
1 teaspoon ground turmeric
1 teaspoon cayenne pepper
2 tablespoons tomato paste
2 x 400g cans diced tomatoes
2 cups (500ml) water
2 x 420g cans chickpeas, rinsed, drained
1 large kumara (500g), cut into 1.5cm pieces
300g spinach, trimmed, chopped coarsely

1   Heat ghee in large saucepan; cook seeds, stirring, until fragrant. Add onion, garlic and ginger; cook, stirring, until onion softens. Add spices; cook, stirring, until fragrant. Add tomato paste; cook, stirring, 2 minutes.
2   Add undrained tomatoes, the water, chickpeas and kumara; simmer, covered, stirring occasionally, about 30 minutes or until kumara is tender and mixture thickens slightly.
3   Stir in spinach just before serving.
__ per serving 8.1g total fat (4.1g saturated fat); 1037kJ (248 cal); 29.1g carbohydrate; 9.9g protein; 9.4g fibre

This recipe gets its heat from the cayenne, the ground dried pods of a special variety of pungent chilli. Vegetarians will be delighted with the chickpeas as a main course served with raita, and Indian breads such as chapati, poori or paratha.

preparation time 15 minutes cooking time 45 minutes serves 6

cauliflower and green pea curry

1 Boil, steam or microwave cauliflower until just tender; drain.
2 Meanwhile, heat ghee in large saucepan; cook onion, garlic and ginger, stirring, until onion softens. Add paste; cook, stirring, until mixture is fragrant.
3 Add cream; bring to a boil then reduce heat. Add cauliflower and tomato; simmer, uncovered, 5 minutes, stirring occasionally.
4 Add peas and yogurt; stir over low heat about 5 minutes or until peas are just cooked. Serve curry sprinkled with egg and coriander.
__ per serving 40.9g total fat (21.9g saturated fat); 2132kJ (510 cal); 15.5g carbohydrate; 17g protein; 8.6g fibre

600g cauliflower florets
2 tablespoons ghee
1 medium brown onion (150g), chopped finely
2 cloves garlic, crushed
2cm piece fresh ginger (10g), grated
¼ cup (75g) hot curry paste
¾ cup (180ml) cream
2 large tomatoes (440g), chopped coarsely
1 cup (120g) frozen peas
1 cup (280g) yogurt
3 hard-boiled eggs, sliced thinly
¼ cup finely chopped fresh coriander

Cauliflower is a popular choice for vegetarian curries because it's both filling and, while it has a great taste of its own, the texture of the florets captures the sauce. In this recipe we used vindaloo paste, but any hot curry paste (red curry paste, for example) would work just as well.

preparation time 20 minutes cooking time 30 minutes serves 4

pumpkin and bean curry

2 teaspoons ground cumin
2 teaspoons ground ginger
1 teaspoon ground coriander
1 tablespoon peanut oil
4 fresh long red chillies, sliced thinly
10cm stick (20g) fresh lemon grass,
  sliced thinly
2 cloves garlic, crushed
4 fresh kaffir lime leaves, shredded finely
1 medium red onion (170g), sliced thinly
2 x 400ml cans coconut milk
⅓ cup (80ml) lime juice
1 tablespoon kecap asin
1 tablespoon grated palm sugar
1kg butternut pumpkin, chopped coarsely
250g sugar snap peas, trimmed
200g snake beans, trimmed,
  chopped coarsely
1 cup (140g) coarsely chopped roasted
  unsalted peanuts
½ cup firmly packed fresh coriander leaves

1 Dry-fry spices in wok over medium heat, stirring, about 1 minute or until fragrant. Add oil, chilli, lemon grass, garlic, lime leaves and onion; stir-fry until onion softens.
2 Add coconut milk, juice, kecap asin, sugar and pumpkin; simmer, uncovered, about 20 minutes or until pumpkin softens. Stir in peas and beans; cook, uncovered, about 5 minutes or until vegetables are just tender.
3 Serve curry sprinkled with nuts and fresh coriander.
— per serving 64.2g total fat (39.7g saturated fat); 3436kJ (822 cal); 34.9g carbohydrate; 21.7g protein; 12.9g fibre

To make this curry from Thailand even hotter, slice the unseeded red chillies into long strips, then dry-fry them on their own, before starting to roast the spices, stirring constantly, until they are crisp and almost blackened. Their colour, crunch and taste will be awesome – albeit hot.

preparation time 30 minutes cooking time 35 minutes serves 4

mixed dhal

1 Heat ghee in large saucepan; cook onion, garlic and ginger, stirring, until onion softens. Add seeds, chilli and spices; cook, stirring, until fragrant.

2 Add lentils and peas to pan. Stir in undrained tomatoes, stock and the water; simmer, covered, stirring occasionally, about 1 hour or until lentils are tender.

3 Just before serving, add coconut cream; stir over low heat until curry is heated through.

— per serving 18.4g total fat (12.5g saturated fat); 1898kJ (454 cal); 42.6g carbohydrate; 23.3g protein; 12.7g fibre

2 tablespoons ghee
1 medium brown onion (150g), chopped finely
2 cloves garlic, crushed
4cm piece fresh ginger (20g), grated
1½ tablespoons black mustard seeds
1 long green chilli, chopped finely
1 tablespoon ground cumin
1 tablespoon ground coriander
2 teaspoons ground turmeric
½ cup (100g) brown lentils
⅓ cup (65g) red lentils
⅓ cup (85g) yellow split peas
⅓ cup (85g) green split peas
400g can crushed tomatoes
2 cups (500ml) vegetable stock
1½ cups (375ml) water
140ml can coconut cream

The word dhal is the Hindi word for legumes and pulses; regarded as meat substitutes, they feature widely in Indian cooking because they are a good source of protein for this largely vegetarian nation.

preparation time 15 minutes cooking time 1 hour 10 minutes serves 4

sambal goreng telor

4 fresh long red chillies, chopped coarsely

4 medium brown onions (600g),
   chopped coarsely

4 cloves garlic, quartered

4cm piece fresh galangal (20g),
   chopped coarsely

2 teaspoons vegetable oil

2 teaspoons ground coriander

32 fresh curry leaves

1 tablespoon kecap asin

10 medium tomatoes (1.5kg), peeled,
   seeded, chopped finely

½ cup (140g) tomato paste

1½ cups (375ml) vegetable stock

12 hard-boiled eggs, halved

1 Blend or process chilli, onion, garlic and galangal until smooth. Heat oil in large saucepan; cook chilli mixture, coriander, curry leaves and kecap asin, stirring, about 5 minutes or until fragrant.
2 Stir tomato, tomato paste and stock into mixture; simmer, covered, 30 minutes.
3 Add egg; simmer, covered, until sambal is heated through.
__ per serving 13.5g total fat (3.8g saturated fat); 991kJ (237 cal); 9.4g carbohydrate; 17.9g protein; 3.9g fibre

This traditional Indonesian recipe transcends the basic idea of sambal being just an accompaniment to meals; by adding stock and hard-boiled eggs, it becomes a delicious, fragrant curry in its own right. Eat it with plain steamed rice and some fresh green vegetables for a main course.

preparation time 25 minutes **cooking time** 45 minutes **serves** 6

tofu and vegetable curry

1   Press tofu between two chopping boards with a weight on top, raise one end; stand 10 minutes. Cut tofu into 2cm cubes; pat dry between layers of absorbent paper.

2   Blend or process garlic, chilli, lemon grass, turmeric, ginger, onion and oil until mixture forms a paste.

3   Cook garlic paste in large saucepan, stirring, 5 minutes. Add coconut milk, stock and lime leaves; simmer, uncovered, stirring occasionally, 10 minutes.

4   Add zucchini and cauliflower; simmer, uncovered, about 5 minutes or until vegetables are tender.

5   Discard lime leaves; stir in tofu, sauce, juice and coriander. Sprinkle with basil before serving.

__ per serving 31.7g total fat (19.7g saturated fat); 1843kJ (441 cal); 14.8g carbohydrate; 19.8g protein; 11g fibre

300g firm silken tofu
6 cloves garlic, quartered
3 fresh small red thai chillies,
    chopped coarsely
10cm stick (20g) fresh lemon grass,
    chopped coarsely
1.5cm piece fresh turmeric (20g),
    chopped coarsely
4cm piece fresh ginger (20g),
    chopped coarsely
1 medium brown onion (150g),
    chopped finely
1 tablespoon vegetable oil
400ml can coconut milk
1 cup (250ml) vegetable stock
2 fresh kaffir lime leaves
4 medium zucchini (480g), chopped coarsely
1 small cauliflower (1kg), cut into florets
1 tablespoon soy sauce
1 tablespoon lime juice
⅓ cup firmly packed fresh coriander,
    chopped coarsely
¼ cup loosely packed fresh thai basil leaves

This vegetable recipe is a good example of a typical Thai curry from the south of the country where the food bears the closest similarities to the food of India. The chilli, turmeric, ginger and coconut milk could just as easily be found in a southern Indian vegetable curry as they are in this.

preparation time 25 minutes (plus standing time) cooking time 25 minutes serves 4

accompaniments

Curries are about combining flavours and textures: temper the heat of chilli with a soothing raita, add tang to a fish curry with koshumbir, or serve a vegetable curry with a fragrant rice dish like a classic pulao.

nasi goreng

1 tablespoon peanut oil
2 eggs, beaten lightly
1 teaspoon sesame oil
1 medium brown onion (150g), sliced thinly
4 green onions, sliced thinly
1 clove garlic, crushed
5cm piece fresh ginger (25g), grated
2 cups (160g) shredded chinese cabbage
1 cup (80g) bean sprouts
3 cups cooked white long-grain rice
1 tablespoon sambal oelek
1 tablespoon kecap manis
1 lebanese cucumber (130g), sliced thinly
1 medium tomato (150g), sliced thinly

1 Heat one teaspoon of the peanut oil in large wok; add half the egg mixture, swirl wok to make a thin omelette. Remove from wok; roll omelette into cigar-shape, cut into thin strips. Repeat with one more teaspoon of the peanut oil and remaining egg mixture.
2 Heat remaining peanut oil and sesame oil in wok; stir-fry onions, garlic and ginger until onion softens. Add cabbage and sprouts; stir-fry over high heat until vegetables are just tender.
3 Add rice, omelette, sambal and kecap manis to wok; stir-fry until heated through.
4 Serve nasi goreng with cucumber and tomato.
__ per serving 8.9g total fat (1.8g saturated fat); 1292kJ (302 cal); 45.6g carbohydrate; 9.3g protein; 4.1g fibre

Nasi goreng, which translates as "fried rice" in Bahasa Indonesian and Malaysian, was originally created as a means to use up yesterday's leftovers. If you have no leftover cooked rice, cook 1 cup (200g) white long-grain rice the night before and refrigerate it, spread thinly on a tray, covered, overnight. You'll also need to buy half a chinese cabbage for this recipe.

preparation time 20 minutes cooking time 20 minutes serves 4

koshumbir

preparation time 10 minutes makes 2 cups

1 small brown onion (80g), chopped finely
1 lebanese cucumber (130g), seeded, grated coarsely
1 small carrot (70g), grated coarsely
1 long green chilli, chopped finely
3cm piece fresh ginger (15g), grated
¼ cup (35g) crushed roasted unsalted peanuts
1 tablespoon lemon juice

1 Combine onion, cucumber, carrot, chilli, ginger and nuts in small bowl. Stir juice into koshumbir just before serving.
__ per ¼ cup 2.1g total fat (0.2g saturated fat); 142kJ (34 cal); 1.7g carbohydrate; 1.4g protein; 1g fibre

Koshumbir, sometimes spelled koshambir, is a fresh shredded vegetable salad that is served in India alongside curries.

tomato kasaundi

preparation time 10 minutes
cooking time 50 minutes makes 3 cups

4 large tomatoes (880g), chopped coarsely
1 medium brown onion (150g), chopped coarsely
4 cloves garlic, chopped coarsely
3cm piece fresh ginger (15g), chopped finely
4 fresh small red thai chillies, chopped coarsely
2 teaspoons ground cumin
½ teaspoon ground turmeric
½ teaspoon chilli powder
¼ teaspoon ground clove
2 tablespoons vegetable oil
¼ cup (60ml) white vinegar
⅓ cup (75g) firmly packed brown sugar

1 Blend or process ingredients until smooth. Transfer mixture to large saucepan; cook, stirring, without boiling, until sugar is dissolved.
2 Simmer, uncovered, stirring occasionally, about 45 minutes or until kasaundi thickens slightly.
__ per tablespoon 1.6g total fat (0.2g saturated fat); 142kJ (34 cal); 4.1g carbohydrate; 0.5g protein; 0.6g fibre

This Indian pickle hails from Goa, and is delicious spread on sandwiches or mixed with rice and eaten with curries.

date and tamarind chutney

preparation time 10 minutes
cooking time 45 minutes makes 2½ cups

2 cinnamon sticks
5 cardamom pods, bruised
2 teaspoons cloves
3½ cups (500g) seeded dried dates
1½ cups (375ml) white vinegar
½ cup (110g) firmly packed brown sugar
2 teaspoons coarse cooking salt
¼ cup (60ml) vegetable oil
2 tablespoons tamarind concentrate
2 teaspoons chilli powder

1   Place cinnamon, cardamom and cloves in centre
of 20cm muslin square; tie tightly with kitchen string.
2   Combine muslin bag with remaining ingredients
in large saucepan; bring to a boil, stirring constantly,
then reduce heat.
3   Simmer, partially covered, stirring occasionally, about
40 minutes or until dates are soft. Remove and discard
spice bag before using.
__ per tablespoon 1.9g total fat (0.2g saturated fat); 343kJ
(82 cal); 15g carbohydrate; 0.4g protein; 1.7g fibre

eggplant chutney

preparation time 10 minutes (plus standing time)
cooking time 55 minutes makes 3 cups

1 medium eggplant (300g), peeled, chopped coarsely
¼ cup (70g) coarse cooking salt
1 medium brown onion (150g), chopped coarsely
2 medium tomatoes (300g), seeded, chopped coarsely
1 small green capsicum (150g), chopped coarsely
2 cloves garlic, crushed
½ cup (125ml) cider vinegar
½ cup (125ml) white vinegar
1 teaspoon chilli powder
1 teaspoon ground turmeric
½ cup (110g) firmly packed brown sugar

1   Place eggplant in colander, sprinkle with salt; stand
30 minutes. Rinse eggplant, pat dry.
2   Combine eggplant, onion, tomato, capsicum, garlic,
vinegars, chilli and turmeric in large saucepan; simmer,
uncovered, stirring occasionally, about 45 minutes or
until vegetables are pulpy.
3   Stir in sugar; cook, stirring, over low heat, until
sugar dissolves.
__ per tablespoon 0.0g total fat (0.0g saturated fat); 67kJ
(16 cal); 3.5g carbohydrate; 0.3g protein; 0.3g fibre

This is a delicious
tangy Indian relish
that goes well with
meaty curries or
spread on sandwiches
for a burst of flavour.

This chutney is quick
and easy to make,
and will keep under
refrigeration for up
to three months in
a sterilised jar.

yellow coconut rice with serundeng

The subtle flavour of this rich, savoury rice from the south of Thailand makes a good accompaniment to more highly spiced dishes. Serundeng, an Indonesian condiment, is usually sprinkled over a hot dish just as it's served, much like a gremolata, to awaken the tastebuds. It's good served with vegetable curries as well as rice dishes like this.

1 Soak rice in large bowl of cold water 30 minutes. Pour rice into strainer; rinse under cold water until water runs clear. Drain.
2 Meanwhile, make serundeng.
3 Place rice and remaining ingredients in large heavy-based saucepan; cover, bring to a boil, stirring occasionally, then reduce heat. Simmer, covered, about 15 minutes or until rice is tender. Remove from heat; stand, covered, 5 minutes, before serving.
SERUNDENG Preheat oven to slow (150°C/130°C fan-forced). Heat oil in wok; stir-fry remaining ingredients, tossing constantly, about 15 minutes or until browned lightly. Transfer mixture to oven tray; cook, uncovered, about 20 minutes or until serundeng has dried.
TIP Any leftover serundeng can be stored in a glass jar in the refrigerator for up to a month.
__ per serving 71.3g total fat (43.4g saturated fat); 4615kJ (1104 cal); 91.6g carbohydrate; 19.4g protein; 11.9g fibre

1¾ cups (350g) white long-grain rice
400ml can coconut cream
1¼ cups (310ml) water
1 teaspoon caster sugar
½ teaspoon ground turmeric
pinch saffron threads
SERUNDENG
2 tablespoons peanut oil
2 cloves garlic, crushed
4 green onions, chopped finely
3 cups (150g) flaked coconut
2 tablespoons brown sugar
½ cup (150g) tamarind concentrate
10cm stick (20g) fresh lemon grass, chopped finely
1 cup (140g) roasted unsalted peanuts

preparation time 5 minutes (plus standing time) cooking time 25 minutes serves 4

vietnamese carrot pickle (nuoc cham)

1 Combine ingredients in medium bowl.
__ per serving 0.0g total fat (0.0g saturated fat); 79kJ (19 cal); 4.1g carbohydrate; 0.4g protein; 0.3g fibre

1 clove garlic, crushed
1 fresh long red chilli, chopped finely
¼ cup (60ml) lime juice
¼ cup (60ml) fish sauce
¼ cup (65g) grated palm sugar
½ cup (125ml) water
1 medium carrot (120g), grated coarsely

preparation time 10 minutes makes 1½ cups

cucumber raita

preparation time 5 minutes
cooking time 2 minutes serves 6

2 teaspoons vegetable oil
¼ teaspoon black mustard seeds
¼ teaspoon cumin seeds
2 lebanese cucumbers (260g), seeded, chopped finely
500g yogurt

1   Heat oil in small frying pan; cook seeds, stirring, over low heat, 2 minutes or until seeds pop.
2   Combine seeds and remaining ingredients in medium bowl; mix well.
__ per serve 4.4g total fat (2g saturated fat); 314kJ (75 cal); 4.5g carbohydrate; 4.1g protein; 0.4g fibre

mint raita

preparation time 5 minutes
cooking time 2 minutes serves 6

2 teaspoons vegetable oil
¼ teaspoon black mustard seeds
¼ teaspoon ground cumin
1 cup finely chopped fresh mint
500g yogurt

1   Heat oil in small frying pan; cook spices, stirring, over low heat, 2 minutes or until seeds pop.
2   Combine spices and remaining ingredients in medium bowl; mix well.
__ per serve 4.5g total fat (2g saturated fat); 314kJ (75 cal); 4.3g carbohydrate; 4.2g protein; 0.6g fibre

Raita translates as yogurt, and when seasoned with vegetables, fruits or spices, it makes a wonderful cooling accompaniment to fiery curries. Leaving raitas to stand 30 minutes before serving allows their flavours to blend more intensely.

carrot raita

preparation time 5 minutes
cooking time 2 minutes serves 6

2 teaspoons vegetable oil
5 fresh curry leaves, chopped finely
1 teaspoon black mustard seeds
1 dried small red chilli, chopped finely
2 medium carrots (240g), grated coarsely
250g yogurt

1   Heat oil in small frying pan; cook leaves and spices, stirring, over low heat, 2 minutes or until seeds pop.
2   Combine leaves, spices and remaining ingredients in medium bowl; mix well.
__ per serving 4.4g total fat (2g saturated fat); 347kJ (83 cal); 6.1g carbohydrate; 4.2g protein; 1.2g fibre

spinach raita

preparation time 5 minutes
cooking time 5 minutes serves 4

500g spinach
¾ cup (210g) yogurt
1 teaspoon lemon juice
½ teaspoon ground cumin
½ teaspoon caster sugar

1   Boil, steam or microwave spinach until just wilted; drain, squeeze out excess liquid.
2   Blend or process spinach with remaining ingredients until smooth.
__ per serve 2.2g total fat (1.2g saturated fat); 263kJ (63 cal); 3.8g carbohydrate; 5.5g protein; 3.4g fibre

Khitcherie, a classic Indian rice and lentil dish, was anglicised by the Raj to make that English breakfast staple, kedgeree. Commercial garam masala, found in some supermarkets, can be used instead of making our recipe.

1 cup (200g) yellow split peas
2 tablespoons ghee
1 medium brown onion (150g), chopped finely
2 cloves garlic, crushed
2 long green chillies, sliced thinly
3cm piece fresh ginger (15g), grated
½ teaspoon ground turmeric
1 teaspoon cumin seeds
½ teaspoon garam masala (page 112)
1 teaspoon ground coriander
1 cinnamon stick
4 fresh curry leaves
1½ cups (300g) basmati rice, rinsed, drained
1 cup (150g) raisins
1 litre (4 cups) hot water
1 tablespoon lime juice
½ cup (75g) roasted unsalted cashews

khitcherie

1 Place split peas in small bowl; cover with cold water, stand 1 hour, drain.
2 Heat ghee in large deep frying pan; cook onion, garlic, chilli, ginger, spices and curry leaves, stirring, until onion softens.
3 Add peas, rice, raisins and the hot water to pan; bring to a boil then reduce heat. Simmer, covered, about 15 minutes or until rice is tender.
4 Remove from heat, discard cinnamon stick, stir in juice; stand, covered, 5 minutes. Sprinkle khitcherie with nuts before serving.
— per serving 13.2g total fat (5.1g saturated fat); 2073kJ (496 cal); 76.3g carbohydrate; 14.3g protein; 6.5g fibre

preparation time 15 minutes (plus standing time) **cooking time** 20 minutes **serves** 6

Pulao, pilaf, pilav or pellao, all are the same cooked grain (usually rice) dish having different spellings in their respective countries of origin. The secret of a perfect pulao is to rinse the grain thoroughly, to remove excess starch, then soak it briefly. Soaking before cooking softens the grains and results in a fluffier pulao.

1⅓ cups (265g) basmati rice, rinsed, drained
2½ cups (625ml) chicken stock
pinch saffron threads
50g butter
1 medium brown onion (150g), chopped finely
2 cloves garlic, crushed
1 cinnamon stick
6 cardamom pods
1 bay leaf
⅓ cup (55g) sultanas
½ cup (75g) roasted unsalted cashews

classic pulao

1 Place rice in medium bowl, cover with cold water; stand 20 minutes, drain.
2 Heat stock and saffron in small saucepan.
3 Meanwhile, melt butter in large saucepan; cook onion and garlic, stirring, until onion softens. Stir in cinnamon, cardamom and bay leaf; cook, stirring, 2 minutes.
4 Add rice; cook, stirring, 2 minutes. Add stock mixture and sultanas; simmer, covered, about 10 minutes or until rice is tender and liquid is absorbed.
5 Sprinkle pulao with nuts just before serving.
— per serving 20.6g total fat (8.8g saturated fat); 2128kJ (509 cal); 68.7g carbohydrate; 10.5g protein; 3g fibre

preparation time 10 minutes (plus standing time) **cooking time** 20 minutes **serves** 4

curry pastes

Commercial curry pastes can't compare to the amazing blend of flavours and explosion of taste and aroma created by homemade ones; however, they do save time and probably, in the end, money. Jars of Thai and Indian curry pastes, as well as garam masala and curry powder are available in most supermarkets, but you may have to adjust the amounts used to those called for in our recipes. Most of these recipes make one cup; use the amount required in each curry then freeze the rest, in one tablespoon batches, for up to three months.

green curry paste

2 teaspoons ground coriander
2 teaspoons ground cumin
10 long green chillies, chopped coarsely
10 small green chillies, chopped coarsely
1 teaspoon shrimp paste
1 clove garlic, quartered
4 green onions, chopped coarsely
10cm stick (20g) fresh lemon grass,
  finely chopped
1cm piece fresh galangal (5g),
  chopped finely
¼ cup coarsely chopped fresh coriander
  root and stem mixture
1 tablespoon peanut oil

preparation time 20 minutes
cooking time 3 minutes **makes** 1 cup

1 Dry-fry ground coriander and cumin in small frying pan over medium heat, stirring until fragrant.
2 Blend or process spices with chillies, paste, garlic, onion, lemon grass, galangal and coriander mixture until mixture forms a paste.
3 Add oil to paste; continue to blend until smooth.
— per tablespoon 1.6g total fat (0.3g saturated fat); 67kJ (16 cal); 0.3g carbohydrate; 0.2g protein; 0.2g fibre

red curry paste

20 dried long red chillies
1 teaspoon ground coriander
2 teaspoons ground cumin
1 teaspoon hot paprika
2cm piece fresh ginger (10g),
  chopped finely
3 cloves garlic, quartered
1 medium red onion (170g),
  chopped coarsely
2 x 10cm sticks (40g) fresh lemon grass,
  thinly sliced
2 tablespoons coarsely chopped fresh
  coriander root and stem mixture
2 teaspoons shrimp paste
1 tablespoon peanut oil

preparation time 20 minutes (plus standing time)
cooking time 5 minutes **makes** 1 cup

1 Place chillies in small heatproof jug, cover with boiling water; stand 15 minutes, drain.
2 Meanwhile, dry-fry ground coriander, cumin and paprika in small frying pan, stirring until fragrant.
3 Blend or process chillies and spices with ginger, garlic, onion, lemon grass, coriander mixture and paste until mixture forms a paste.
4 Add oil to paste; continue to blend until smooth.
— per tablespoon 1.6g total fat (0.3g saturated fat); 92kJ (22 cal); 1.2g carbohydrate; 0.4g protein; 0.5g fibre

tandoori paste

preparation time 15 minutes
cooking time 5 minutes makes ½ cup

Tandoori paste is a highly-seasoned classic East Indian marinade used to give foods the authentic red-orange tint of tandoor oven cooking.

1   Dry-fry seeds in small frying pan over medium heat, stirring until fragrant.
2   Blend or process seeds with remaining ingredients until smooth.

__ per tablespoon 0.1g total fat (0.0g saturated fat); 25kJ (6 cal); 0.7g carbohydrate; 0.3g protein; 0.6g fibre

2 teaspoons cumin seeds
2 teaspoons coriander seeds
1 teaspoon cardamom seeds
2 teaspoons garam masala
½ teaspoon chilli powder
1 teaspoon cracked black pepper
3 cloves garlic, crushed
2cm piece fresh ginger (10g), chopped finely
1 fresh long red chilli, chopped finely
¼ cup (60ml) lemon juice
½ cup firmly packed fresh coriander leaves
1¼ teaspoons red food colouring
¾ teaspoon yellow food colouring

panang curry paste

preparation time 20 minutes (plus standing time)
cooking time 3 minutes makes 1 cup

1   Place chillies in small heatproof jug, cover with boiling water; stand 15 minutes, drain.
2   Meanwhile, dry-fry coriander and cumin in small frying pan over medium heat, stirring until fragrant.
3   Blend or process chillies and spices with remaining ingredients until mixture forms a paste.

__ per tablespoon 6.1g total fat (0.9g saturated fat); 288kJ (69 cal); 1.3g carbohydrate; 1.9g protein; 0.9g fibre

25 dried long red chillies
1 teaspoon ground coriander
2 teaspoons ground cumin
2 cloves garlic, quartered
8 green onions, chopped coarsely
2 x 10cm sticks (40g) fresh lemon grass, thinly sliced
2cm piece fresh galangal (10g), chopped finely
2 teaspoons shrimp paste
½ cup (75g) roasted unsalted peanuts
2 tablespoons peanut oil

yellow curry paste

preparation time 20 minutes (plus standing time)
cooking time 3 minutes makes 1 cup

1   Place chillies in small heatproof jug, cover with boiling water; stand 15 minutes, drain.
2   Meanwhile, dry-fry ground coriander, cumin and cinnamon in small frying pan, stirring until fragrant.
3   Blend or process spices and chillies with remaining ingredients until mixture is smooth.

__ per tablespoon 1.6g total fat (0.3g saturated fat); 84kJ (20 cal); 0.9g carbohydrate; 0.4g protein; 0.5g fibre

2 dried long red chillies
1 teaspoon ground coriander
1 teaspoon ground cumin
½ teaspoon ground cinnamon
2 fresh yellow banana chillies (250g), chopped coarsely
1 teaspoon finely chopped fresh turmeric
2 cloves garlic, quartered
1 small brown onion (80g), chopped finely
10cm stick (20g) fresh lemon grass, finely chopped
2 teaspoons finely chopped fresh galangal
1 tablespoon coarsely chopped fresh coriander root and stem mixture
1 teaspoon shrimp paste
1 tablespoon peanut oil

garam masala

1 tablespoon fennel seeds
2 teaspoons ground cinnamon
1 teaspoon ground cardamom
1 teaspoon cracked black pepper
½ teaspoon ground clove
1 bay leaf

preparation time 10 minutes **cooking time** 5 minutes
makes about 2 tablespoons

Garam masala, an essential spice if you're a fan of Indian food, is a mixture of several ground spices added to a dish near the end of cooking to give aroma and flavour. Mix it with a little water and add to curries or sprinkle it over a dish as a seasoning.

1 Dry-fry ingredients in small frying pan, stirring until fragrant.
2 Blend or process mixture, or crush using mortar and pestle, until mixture is ground coarsely.
__ per tablespoon 0.3g total fat (0.0g saturated fat); 54kJ (13 cal); 1.2g carbohydrate; 0.3g protein; 0.2g fibre

chilli sauce

10 fresh long red chillies, chopped coarsely
1¼ cups (310ml) water
1 tablespoon white vinegar
1 tablespoon caster sugar

preparation time 10 minutes
cooking time 15 minutes **makes** 1¼ cups

1 Place chilli and the water in small saucepan, bring to a boil, then reduce heat. Simmer, uncovered, 15 minutes.
2 Stir in vinegar and sugar. Blend or process until smooth.
__ per tablespoon 0.0g total fat (0.0g saturated fat); 21kJ (5 cal); 1.2g carbohydrate; 0.0g protein; 0.1g fibre

roasted curry powder

10cm stick (20g) fresh lemon grass,
   chopped finely
1 cinnamon stick
½ cup (40g) coriander seeds
10 fresh curry leaves
2 cardamom pods
3 cloves
¼ cup (40g) cumin seeds
¼ cup (30g) fennel seeds

preparation time 10 minutes
cooking time 5 minutes **makes** 1 cup

This blend of spices, when rubbed over meats before cooking, gives an authentic Indian taste to food.

1 Cook lemon grass and cinnamon in medium frying pan, stirring, over medium heat, about 3 minutes or until lemon grass turns golden brown. Add coriander seeds, curry leaves, cardamom and cloves; cook, stirring about 1 minute or until fragrant.
2 Remove pan from heat; stir in cumin and fennel seeds.
3 Blend or process mixture until reduced to a powder.
__ per tablespoon 0.0g total fat (0.0g saturated fat); 8kJ (2 cal); 0.3g carbohydrate; 0.0g protein; 0.3g fibre

massaman curry paste

preparation time 15 minutes (plus standing time)
cooking time 20 minutes **makes** 1 cup

1 Preheat oven to moderate (180°C/160°C fan-forced).
2 Place chillies in small heatproof jug, cover with boiling water; stand 15 minutes, drain.
3 Meanwhile, dry-fry coriander, cumin, cinnamon, cardamom and clove in small frying pan, stirring until fragrant.
4 Place chillies and spices in small shallow baking dish with remaining ingredients. Roast, uncovered, 15 minutes.
5 Blend or process roasted curry paste mixture, or crush using mortar and pestle, until smooth.
__ per tablespoon 1.7g total fat (0.3g saturated fat); 105kJ (25 cal); 1.5g carbohydrate; 0.5g protein; 0.4g fibre

20 dried long red chillies
1 teaspoon ground coriander
2 teaspoons ground cumin
2 teaspoons ground cinnamon
½ teaspoon ground cardamom
½ teaspoon ground clove
5 cloves garlic, quartered
1 large brown onion (200g), chopped coarsely
2 x 10cm sticks (40g) fresh lemon grass, thinly sliced
3 fresh kaffir lime leaves, sliced thinly
4cm piece fresh ginger (20g), chopped coarsely
2 teaspoons shrimp paste
1 tablespoon peanut oil

laksa paste

preparation time 20 minutes **makes** 1 cup

1 Place chillies in small heatproof jug, cover with boiling water; stand 10 minutes; drain.
2 Blend or process chillies with remaining ingredients until mixture is smooth.
__ per tablespoon 2.3g total fat (0.4g saturated fat); 109kJ (26 cal); 26.4g carbohydrate; 0.4g protein; 0.5g fibre

7 dried small red chillies
1 tablespoon peanut oil
3 cloves garlic, quartered
1 medium brown onion (150g), chopped coarsely
10cm stick (20g) fresh lemon grass, chopped finely
4cm piece fresh ginger (20g), grated
1 tablespoon coarsely chopped macadamias
2 tablespoons coarsely chopped fresh coriander root and stem mixture
1 teaspoon ground turmeric
1 teaspoon ground coriander
½ cup loosely packed fresh vietnamese mint leaves

glossary

ALLSPICE also known as pimento or jamaican pepper; available whole or ground. So-named because it tastes like a combination of nutmeg, cumin, clove and cinnamon – all spices.

ALMONDS flat, pointed ended nuts with pitted brown shell enclosing a creamy white kernel that is covered by a brown skin.
blanched brown skins removed.
slivered small lengthways-cut pieces.

ARROWROOT a starch used mostly for thickening. Cornflour can be substituted, but it will not give as clear a glaze.

BABY CORN small corn cobs canned in brine; available from most Asian food stores.

BAMBOO SHOOTS young edible shoots of various types of bamboo; pale yellow, crunchy and fibrous, available fresh from Asian food shops and greengrocers, as well as peeled, sliced, cooked and canned from supermarkets. Rinse the canned variety well to rid the shoots of all traces of can liquid. *(see page 44)*

BASIL
opal has large purple leaves and a sweet, almost gingery flavour; can be used instead of thai basil, but not holy basil, in recipes.
holy also known as kra pao or hot basil; has a hot, spicy flavour similar to clove.

BAY LEAVES aromatic leaves from the bay tree; used to add flavour to dishes.

BEANS
snake beans long (about 40cm), thin, round, fresh green beans, Asian in origin, with a taste similar to green or french beans.
sprouts also known as bean shoots; tender new growths of assorted beans and seeds germinated for consumption as sprouts.

BLUE-EYE thick, moist, white-fleshed fish also known as deep-sea trevalla or trevally and blue-eye cod.

BOK CHOY also known as bak choy, pak choy, chinese white cabbage or chinese chard, has a fresh, mild mustard taste; use stems and leaves.

baby bok choy also known as shanghai bok choy, chinese chard, white cabbage or pak kat farang, is small and more tender than bok choy.

BUTTERMILK sold in the refrigerated dairy compartments in supermarkets. Despite the implication of its name, it is low in fat.

CAPSICUM also known as bell pepper or, simply, pepper. Discard seeds and membranes before use.

CAULIFLOWER cruciferous vegetable with a white, purple or green edible floret portion, called the "curd". Choose a firm cauliflower with compact florets; leaves should be crisp and green with no signs of yellowing.

CHAPATI one of a number of flat breads from India that also include naan, phulka and roti, poori and parantha; made of flour and water.

CHICKPEAS also called garbanzos, hummus or channa; an irregularly round, sandy-coloured legume.

CHILLI use rubber gloves when seeding and chopping fresh chillies as they can burn your skin. To lessen the heat level, remove the seeds and membranes.
banana long and tapering, they are also known as wax chillies, hungarian peppers or sweet banana peppers. They are almost as mild as capsicum, but have a slightly sweet sharpness about their taste. They can be pale olive green, yellow or red in colour.
cayenne a thin-fleshed, extremely hot, dried, long red chilli, usually purchased ground.
dried flakes deep-red, dehydrated, extremely fine slices and whole seeds.
green generally unripened thai chillies, but sometimes varieties that are ripe when green, such as habañero, are used.
jalapeños medium length but slightly rounder than an average long chilli; can be medium to hot in flavour.
powder made from dried ground thai chillies; can be used as a substitute for fresh chillies in the proportion of ½ teaspoon ground chilli powder to 1 medium chopped fresh chilli.
sweet chilli sauce *see sauces.*

thai small, medium hot, and bright red in colour.

CHINESE CABBAGE this is the most common cabbage in South-East Asia, it is elongated in shape with pale green, crinkly leaves. Also known as peking or napa cabbage, wong bok or petsai.

CHOY SUM also known as pakaukeo or flowering cabbage; has long stems, light green leaves and yellow flowers.

COCONUT
cream made commercially from the first pressing of the coconut flesh alone, without the addition of water. Available at supermarkets in cans and cartons.
desiccated finely shredded strips of concentrated, unsweetened coconut.
flakes dried flaked coconut flesh.
milk diluted liquid from the second pressing from the white meat of a mature coconut. Available in cans and cartons at supermarkets.
shredded thin strips of dried coconut.

CORNFLOUR a thickening agent used in cooking, also known as cornstarch.

CREAM, SOUR a thick, commercially cultured soured cream.

CREME FRAICHE mature fermented cream having a slightly tangy, nutty flavour and velvety texture.

CUCUMBER, LEBANESE short, thin-skinned and slender; also known as the european or burpless cucumber.

CUMIN also known as zeera or comino; the dried seed of a plant related to the parsley family having a spicy, nutty flavour. Available in seed form or dried and ground.

CURRANTS tiny, almost black, raisins.

EGGS some recipes in this book call for raw or barely cooked eggs; exercise caution if there is a salmonella problem in your area.

FENNEL SEEDS dried seeds having a licorice flavour.

FIVE-SPICE POWDER a fragrant mix of cloves, ground cinnamon, star anise, sichuan pepper and fennel seeds. Also known as chinese five-spice.

FLOUR

plain an all-purpose flour, made from wheat.

self-raising plain flour that has been sifted with baking powder in the proportion of 1 cup flour to 2 teaspoons baking powder.

FRENCH-TRIMMED trimmed lamb shanks, sold as frenched shanks or sometimes lamb drumsticks, have had the upper ends of the bones trimmed short and scraped, while the shank meat itself has been trimmed of excess fat, membrane and sinew.

FRIED SHALLOTS (homm jiew) can be purchased packaged in jars or cellophane bags at Asian grocery stores; once opened, they keep for months if stored tightly sealed. You can make your own by frying thinly sliced peeled shallots until golden-brown and crisp.

GAI LARN also known as chinese broccoli, kanah, chinese kale and gai lum; appreciated more for its stems than its coarse leaves.

GELATINE available powdered or as sheet form known as leaf gelatine.

GINGER also known as green or root ginger; thick gnarled root of a tropical plant. Can be peeled, covered with dry sherry in a jar and refrigerated, or frozen in an airtight container. Ground ginger cannot be substituted for root ginger. *(see page 36)*

GOW-GEE WRAPPERS also known as gow-gee pastry. Spring roll, egg pastry sheets or wonton wrappers can be substituted.

GRAVY BEEF boneless stewing beef that, when slow cooked, imbues stocks, soups and casseroles with a mild yet aromatic flavour.

KITCHEN STRING be certain to use an all-cotton string and not one made from synthetic material.

KUMARA orange-fleshed sweet potato often confused with yam *(see page 39)*

LENTILS (red, brown, yellow) dried pulses often identified by and named after their colour. *(see page 95)*

LING a member of the cod family with white, firm, moist flesh; fillets are nearly boneless.

MINCE also known as ground meat as in beef, pork, lamb, veal and chicken.

MUSHROOMS

button small, cultivated white mushrooms with a mild flavour.

oyster also known as abalone; grey-white mushroom shaped like a fan. Prized for their smooth texture and subtle, oyster-like flavour.

shiitake when fresh are also known as golden oak, forest or chinese black mushrooms; although cultivated, have the earthiness and taste of wild mushrooms. When dried, are known as donko or dried chinese mushrooms; must be rehydrated before use.

straw also known as paddy straw or grass mushrooms; seldom available fresh, but easily found canned or dried in Asian grocery stores. Have an intense earthy flavour.

MUSTARD SEEDS

black also known as brown mustard seeds; more pungent than the white (or yellow) seeds used in most prepared mustards. *(see page 71)*

NEW POTATOES also known as chats; not a separate variety, but an early harvest with very thin skin. Ranges in size, baby is the first picking.

NUTMEG dried nut of an evergreen tree native to Indonesia; it is available in ground form or you can grate your own with a fine grater.

OIL

olive made from ripened olives. *Extra virgin* and *virgin* are the first and second press, while *extra light* and *light* are diluted, and refer to taste levels not fat levels.

peanut made from ground peanuts; most commonly used oil in Asian cooking because of its high smoke point (capacity to handle high heat without burning).

sesame made from roasted, crushed, white sesame seeds; a flavouring rather than a cooking medium.

vegetable oils sourced from plants rather than animal fats.

ONION

brown is interchangeable with the white onion. Its pungent flesh adds flavour to a vast range of dishes.

green also known as scallion or, incorrectly, shallot; an immature onion picked before the bulb has formed, having a long, bright-green edible stalk.

red also known as spanish, red spanish or bermuda onion; a large, sweet-flavoured, purple-red onion.

shallot also called french shallot, golden shallot or eschalot; small, elongated, brown-skinned members of the onion family. Grows in clusters similar to garlic.

PAPRIKA ground dried red capsicum (bell pepper); available smoked, sweet or hot.

PARSLEY, FLAT-LEAF also known as continental or italian parsley.

PATTY-PAN SQUASH also known as crookneck or custard marrow pumpkins; a round, slightly flat, yellow to pale green summer squash with a scalloped edge.

PEPPERCORNS

black picked when the berry is not quite ripe, then dried until it shrivels and the skin turns dark brown to black. It's the strongest flavoured of all the peppercorn varieties.

POPPY SEEDS possess a nutty, slightly sweet flavour and a dark blue-grey colour.

PRAWNS also known as shrimp.

QUAIL small (250g-300g), delicate flavoured, domestically grown game birds; also known as partridge.

RICE

basmati a white, fragrant long-grained rice that is usually associated with the food of India. It should be washed several times before cooking.

long-grain elongated grain, remains separate when cooked.

medium-grain previously sold as calrose rice, extremely versatile rice that can be substituted for short- or long-grain rices if necessary.

white hulled and polished, can be short- or long-grained.

SAFFRON stigma of a member of the crocus family, it is available in strands or ground form. Once infused, it imparts a yellow-orange colour to food. Should be stored in the freezer.

SAUCES
ground bean sauce a mixture of soy beans, flour, salt, sugar and water.
hoisin a thick, sweet and spicy chinese sauce made from salted fermented soy beans, garlic and onions. Used as a baste, marinade or in stir-fries.
oyster Asian in origin, this rich, brown sauce is made from oysters and their brine, cooked with salt and soy sauce, and thickened with starches.
soy also known as sieu; is made from fermented soy beans. Several types are available in most supermarkets and Asian food stores.
sweet chilli the comparatively mild thai sauce made from red chillies, sugar, garlic and vinegar; used more as a condiment than in cooking.

SCALLOPS a bivalve mollusc with fluted shell valve; we use scallops having the coral (roe) attached.

SILVER BEET also known as swiss chard and mistakenly called spinach; a member of the beet family grown for its tasty green leaves and celery-like stems. Best cooked rather than eaten raw.

SNOW PEAS also called mange tout ("eat all").
snow pea tendrils the growing shoots of the plant, are sold by greengrocers.
snow pea sprouts tender new growths of snow peas; also known as mange tout.

SPINACH known as english spinach and, incorrectly, silver beet. Tender green leaves are good uncooked in salads or added to soups, stir-fries and stews just before serving.

SPLIT PEAS also known as field peas; green or yellow pulse grown especially for drying, split in half along a centre seam. (*see page 95*)

STAR ANISE a dried star-shaped pod whose seeds have an astringent aniseed flavour.

STOCK available in cans, bottles or tetra packs, or as cubes or powder. As a guide, 1 teaspoon of stock powder or 1 small crumbled stock cube mixed with 1 cup (250ml) water will give a fairly strong stock. Be aware of the salt and fat content of stocks.

SUGAR
black moist sugar with a fine texture; brown sugar can be substituted.
brown a soft, fine granulated sugar with molasses for colour and flavour.
caster also known as superfine or finely granulated table sugar.
white unless otherwise specified we use coarse, granulated table sugar, also known as crystal sugar.

SUGAR SNAP PEAS also known as honey snap peas; fresh, small and can be eaten whole.

SULTANAS also known as golden raisins; dried seedless white grapes.

TAT SOI a variety of bok choy, also known as rosette bok choy. Dark leafed, developed to grow close to the ground so it is easily protected from frost. Is tougher and requires longer cooking. Available from greengrocers.

THYME a member of the mint family used in Mediterranean countries to flavour meats and sauces. It has tiny grey-green leaves that give off a minty, light-lemon aroma. Dried thyme comes in both leaf and powder form and should be stored in a cool, dark place for up to three months. Fresh thyme should be stored in the refrigerator, wrapped in a damp paper towel and placed in a sealed bag for a few days only. (*see page 40*)

TOFU also known as bean curd, an off-white, custard-like product made from the "milk" of crushed soy beans; comes fresh as soft or firm, and processed as fried or pressed dried sheets.
firm made by compressing bean curd to remove most of the water. Good used in stir fries because it can be tossed without falling apart.
silken refers to the manufacturing method of straining the soy bean liquid through silk.

TOMATO
canned whole peeled tomatoes in natural juices.
cherry also known as tiny tim or tom thumb tomatoes; small and round.
egg also called plum or roma, are smallish, oval-shaped tomatoes.
juice available in cans, bottled and tetra packs from supermarkets.
paste triple-concentrated tomato puree used to flavour soups, stews, sauces and casseroles.
puree canned pureed tomatoes (not tomato paste). Substitute with fresh peeled and pureed tomatoes.

VINEGAR
balsamic originally from Modena, Italy, there are now many balsamic vinegars on the market ranging in pungency and quality depending on how long they have been aged. Quality can be determined up to a point by price; use the most expensive sparingly.
cider made from fermented apples.
rice a colourless vinegar made from fermented rice and flavoured with sugar and salt. Also known as seasoned rice vinegar. Sherry can be used instead.
rice wine made from rice wine lees (sediment), salt and alcohol.
white made from spirit of cane sugar.

WATERCRESS also known as winter rocket, is a slightly peppery, dark-green leaf vegetable.

WONTON WRAPPERS also known as wonton skins; gow gee, egg or spring roll pastry sheets can be substituted. Made of flour, eggs and water and, once filled with meat, can be easily folded and pinched into shape. Look for them wrapped in plastic in the refrigerator section of supermarkets and Asian food shops. Store them in the refrigerator or freezer, but let them come to room temperature before using.

YOGURT we used plain, unflavoured yogurt, unless otherwise specified.

ZUCCHINI also known as courgette; small green, yellow or white vegetable belonging to the squash family.

index

conversion chart

MEASURES

One Australian metric measuring cup holds approximately 250ml; one Australian metric tablespoon holds 20ml; one Australian metric teaspoon holds 5ml.

The difference between one country's measuring cups and another's is within a two- or three-teaspoon variance, and will not affect your cooking results. North America, New Zealand and the United Kingdom use a 15ml tablespoon.

All cup and spoon measurements are level. The most accurate way of measuring dry ingredients is to weigh them. When measuring liquids, use a clear glass or plastic jug with the metric markings.

We use large eggs with an average weight of 60g.

DRY MEASURES

METRIC	IMPERIAL
15g	½oz
30g	1oz
60g	2oz
90g	3oz
125g	4oz (¼lb)
155g	5oz
185g	6oz
220g	7oz
250g	8oz (½lb)
280g	9oz
315g	10oz
345g	11oz
375g	12oz (¾lb)
410g	13oz
440g	14oz
470g	15oz
500g	16oz (1lb)
750g	24oz (1½lb)
1kg	32oz (2lb)

LIQUID MEASURES

METRIC	IMPERIAL
30ml	1 fluid oz
60ml	2 fluid oz
100ml	3 fluid oz
125ml	4 fluid oz
150ml	5 fluid oz (¼ pint/1 gill)
190ml	6 fluid oz
250ml	8 fluid oz
300ml	10 fluid oz (½ pint)
500ml	16 fluid oz
600ml	20 fluid oz (1 pint)
1000ml (1 litre)	1¾ pints

LENGTH MEASURES

METRIC	IMPERIAL
3mm	⅛in
6mm	¼in
1cm	½in
2cm	¾in
2.5cm	1in
5cm	2in
6cm	2½in
8cm	3in
10cm	4in
13cm	5in
15cm	6in
18cm	7in
20cm	8in
23cm	9in
25cm	10in
28cm	11in
30cm	12in (1ft)

OVEN TEMPERATURES

These oven temperatures are only a guide for conventional ovens. For fan-forced ovens, check the manufacturer's manual.

	°C (CELSIUS)	°F (FAHRENHEIT)	GAS MARK
Very slow	120	250	½
Slow	150	275-300	1-2
Moderately slow	160	325	3
Moderate	180	350-375	4-5
Moderately hot	200	400	6
Hot	220	425-450	7-8
Very hot	240	475	9

ARE YOU MISSING SOME OF THE WORLD'S FAVOURITE COOKBOOKS?

The Australian Women's Weekly Cookbooks are available from bookshops, cookshops, supermarkets and other stores all over the world. You can also buy direct from the publisher, using the order form below.

TITLE	RRP	QTY	TITLE	RRP	QTY
Asian, Meals in Minutes	£6.99		Greek Cooking Class	£6.99	
Babies & Toddlers Good Food	£6.99		Healthy Heart Cookbook	£6.99	
Barbecue Meals In Minutes	£6.99		Indian Cooking Class	£6.99	
Basic Cooking Class	£6.99		Japanese Cooking Class	£6.99	
Beginners Cooking Class	£6.99		Kids' Birthday Cakes	£6.99	
Beginners Simple Meals	£6.99		Kids Cooking	£6.99	
Beginners Thai	£6.99		Lean Food	£6.99	
Best Food	£6.99		Low-carb, Low-fat	£6.99	
Best Food Desserts	£6.99		Low-fat Feasts	£6.99	
Best Food Fast	£6.99		Low-fat Food For Life	£6.99	
Best Food Mains	£6.99		Low-fat Meals in Minutes	£6.99	
Cakes Biscuits & Slices	£6.99		Main Course Salads	£6.99	
Cakes Cooking Class	£6.99		Middle Eastern Cooking Class	£6.99	
Caribbean Cooking	£6.99		Midweek Meals in Minutes	£6.99	
Casseroles	£6.99		Muffins, Scones & Breads	£6.99	
Chicken	£6.99		New Casseroles	£6.99	
Chicken Meals in Minutes	£6.99		New Classics	£6.99	
Chinese Cooking Class	£6.99		New Curries	£6.99	
Christmas Cooking	£6.99		New Finger Food	£6.99	
Chocolate	£6.99		Party Food and Drink	£6.99	
Cocktails	£6.99		Pasta Meals in Minutes	£6.99	
Cooking for Friends	£6.99		Potatoes	£6.99	
Creative Cooking on a Budget	£6.99		Salads: Simple, Fast & Fresh	£6.99	
Detox	£6.99		Saucery	£6.99	
Dinner Beef	£6.99		Sauces Salsas & Dressings	£6.99	
Dinner Lamb	£6.99		Sensational Stir-Fries	£6.99	
Dinner Seafood	£6.99		Short-order Cook	£6.99	
Easy Australian Style	£6.99		Slim	£6.99	
Easy Curry	£6.99		Sweet Old Fashioned Favourites	£6.99	
Easy Spanish-Style	£6.99		Thai Cooking Class	£6.99	
Essential Soup	£6.99		Vegetarian Meals in Minutes	£6.99	
Freezer, Meals from the	£6.99		Vegie Food	£6.99	
French Food, New	£6.99		Weekend Cook	£6.99	
Fresh Food for Babies & Toddlers	£6.99		Wicked Sweet Indulgences	£6.99	
Get Real, Make a Meal	£6.99		Wok, Meals in Minutes	£6.99	
Good Food Fast	£6.99				
Great Lamb Cookbook	£6.99		TOTAL COST:	£	

Mr/Mrs/Ms _____

Address _____

_____ Postcode _____

Day time phone _____ Email* (optional) _____

I enclose my cheque/money order for £ _____

or please charge £ _____

to my: ☐ Access ☐ Mastercard ☐ Visa ☐ Diners Club

PLEASE NOTE: WE DO NOT ACCEPT SWITCH OR ELECTRON CARDS

Card number |__|__|__|__|__|__|__|__|__|__|__|__|__|__|__|__|

Expiry date _____ 3 digit security code *(found on reverse of card)* _____

Cardholder's name_____ Signature _____

To order: Mail or fax – photocopy or complete the order form above, and send your credit card details or cheque payable to: Australian Consolidated Press (UK), Moulton Park Business Centre, Red House Road, Moulton Park, Northampton NN3 6AQ, phone (+44) (0) 1604 497531 fax (+44) (0) 1604 497533, e-mail books@acpmedia.co.uk or order online at www.acpuk.com
Non-UK residents: We accept the credit cards listed on the coupon, or cheques, drafts or International Money Orders payable in sterling and drawn on a UK bank. Credit card charges are at the exchange rate current at the time of payment.
Postage and packing UK: Add £1.00 per order plus 50p per book.
Postage and packing overseas: Add £2.00 per order plus £1.00 per book.
All pricing current at time of going to press and subject to change/availability.
Offer ends 31.12.2007

* By including your email address, you consent to receipt of any email regarding this magazine, and other emails which inform you of ACP's other publications, products, services and events, and to promote third party goods and services you may be interested in.